RECO   G

BENEDICT

twelve-step living
and the
rule of benedict

T0154124

RECOVERING
BENEDICT

twelve-step living
and the
rule of benedict

JOHN EDWARD CREAN JR.

Morehouse Publishing
NEW YORK

Unless otherwise noted, the Scripture quotations contained herein are from the New Revised Standard Version Bible, copyright © 1989 by the Division of Christian Education of the National Council of Churches of Christ in the U.S.A. Used by permission. All rights reserved.

Quotations of Benedict's *Rule* are taken from *A Reader's Version of the Rule of Saint Benedict in Inclusive Language*, edited and adapted by Sister Marilyn Schauble, OSB, and Barbara Wojciak, used by permission of the Community of Mount Saint Benedict in Erie, Pennsylvania; and from the translation by Leonard J. Doyle, OSB, *St. Benedict's Rule for Monasteries* (Collegeville MN: Liturgical Press, 1948).

Morehouse Publishing, 19 East 34th Street, New York, NY 10016
Morehouse Publishing is an imprint of Church Publishing Incorporated.
www.churchpublishing.org

Cover design by Paul Soupiset
Typeset by Rose Design

A record of this book is available from the Library of Congress.

ISBN-13: 978-1-64065-326-9 (paperback)
ISBN-13: 978-1-64065-327-6 (ebook)

ACKNOWLEDGMENTS

Recovering Benedict consciously tries to connect the dots between the twelve steps first published in *The Big Book—Alcoholics Anonymous* with the seventy-three chapters of the *Rule of Benedict*. The format of each daily reading is in two parts: first, the appointed daily reading from the *Rule* and then my reflection on it.

Both the text and my reflections rely on English translations of Benedict's *Rule*. With the kind permission of the Community of Mount Saint Benedict in Erie, Pennsylvania, I quote from *A Reader's Version of the Rule of Saint Benedict in Inclusive Language*, edited and adapted by Sister Marilyn Schauble, OSB, and Barbara Wojciak. During many of my reflections, I often quote from the *Rule* as translated by Leonard J. Doyle, OSB, *St. Benedict's Rule for Monasteries* (Collegeville MN: Liturgical Press, 1948). I am grateful to both publishers for permission to quote from their texts, but I owe my greatest debt to Professor Julian G. Plante, late curator of the Hill Monastic Manuscript Microfilm Library at St. John's, Collegeville, Minnesota, who first whetted my appetite for the *Rule of Benedict*.

Julian and I both happened to be giving papers at one of the first annual meetings of the International Medieval Congress at Western Michigan University in 1968. I was talking on Meister Eckhart, and he was doing something or other on Classics. He stood in front of me in an incredibly long lunch line. To pass the time, we started up a conversation. At some point during that conversation, Julian said, "John, I have just the thing for you to work on."

My scholarly publications from that day forward centered on the *Rule of Benedict*. I never looked back at Eckhart again. And my interest in the *Rule* and Benedictine life went well beyond the confines of academe. I became an oblate in the Benedictine Order—all stemming from that one chance lunch-line encounter. That never-ending line drove my life in a new direction—not just my scholarly life but, more importantly, my spiritual life as well.

May God rest the immortal soul of my friend and colleague, Professor Julian G. Plante, PhD. And may each of you who use this little book be inspired by the spirit of Benedict and the serenity of recovery.

INTRODUCTION

Recovering Benedict **was first inspired** by the down-to-earth wisdom of the *Rule of Benedict* (*RB*). Addicts sometimes suffer from more than one addiction at a time. Numerous anonymous twelve-step programs have come into existence to address addictions to alcohol (AA), narcotics (NA), overeating (OA), gambling (GA), sex (SA), and debt (DA) to name but a few. Support groups such as Al-Anon, Alateen, Nar-Anon, S-Anon, and others were created to assist those who are in a relationship with addicts.

In my view, the most effective recovery programs are those based upon the twelve steps first outlined in a work referred to as *The Big Book* or simply *Alcoholics Anonymous* (April 1939). This pioneering methodology suggests addressing addiction "one day at a time." Because of AA, a generous number of daily recovery readers already exist. *Recovering Benedict* also approaches recovery from twelve-step methodology, but from an additional perspective as well. The meditations after each daily reading from the *Rule of Benedict* were written for persons in recovery and those who support their efforts.

Benedict of Nursia (480–547) was an Italian layperson who sought a more authentic spiritual life than was currently available to him in the religious culture of his day. Benedict, often referred to as the "father of Western monasticism," collated various strands of monastic culture and practice into a single coherent document. He created his short handbook to guide others seeking a holier life. For over fifteen centuries now, the *Rule of Benedict* has been translated, adapted, and adopted in far more ways than Benedict could ever have imagined. It is a true classic of Western spirituality.

An equally novel, indeed revolutionary way to deal with the age-old problem of alcoholism appeared with the publication of *Alcoholics Anonymous*. The first edition of 1939 ushered in a fresh way to approach the *disease* of alcoholism. Based on twelve simple yet practical steps and minus moral judgmentalism, this pioneering venture—like the *Rule*—inspired others to translate, adapt, and adopt it to address not only alcoholism but countless other addictions as well.

Basic to all twelve-step programs are values such as rigorous honesty, interdependence with others (through attending meetings and working with a sponsor), accountability, systematic step work, confidentiality, anonymity, persistence, simplicity, self-evaluation, openness to transformation, humility, consideration, and a reliance on one's Higher Power—however one might understand that. In my view, the twelve-step method has met with such enormous success because deeply within its methodology it has both spiritual as well as therapeutic roots.

While most of the basic values espoused by AA certainly existed well before 1939, it took one motivated individual, in consultation with fellow travelers, to pull the various strands together into a new format. And here is where the dots connect for me: it took a sixth-century Italian drawing on earlier experience to create a handbook for Western monasticism; it likewise took a twentieth-century American to pull together a program for people who just wanted wellness, who wanted to recover.

Recovering Benedict came into being because I, too, found healing by relating monastic practice with recovery values. Monastics and non-monastics alike share the same twenty-four hours. Monastics live twenty-four hours of work balanced with prayer; addicts likewise try to live out their lives one day at a time. How we spend our hours are how we spend our days.

A Recovery Prayer

May your reading and reflection
bring you the peace
that passes all understanding.

May you experience all the serenity
that sober living can bring about.

May you come to quiet
and find wholeness.

May you be restored and revived.

And in our moments of reflection,
in our heartfelt prayers,
let us remember the community of souls
struggling along with us.
Amen.

The Twelve Steps (adapted)

1. I admit I am powerless over my dependencies and that my life has gone out of control.
2. I believe in a Higher Power that can restore me to sanity.
3. I surrender my life and my will to my Higher Power.
4. I examine my life as courageously and as completely as I can.
5. I admit to my Higher Power, to myself, and to someone else exactly what I've been doing wrong.
6. I am fully prepared for my Higher Power to remove all my character defects.
7. I humbly ask my Higher Power to remove all my character defects.
8. I list every person I have harmed and am ready to make amends to each and every one of them.
9. I make amends personally to everyone I have harmed wherever possible, unless doing so would cause them or others further harm.
10. I continue examining my life, and whenever I do wrong, promptly admit it.
11. I seek more conscious contact with my Higher Power, asking only for discernment and perseverance.
12. Grateful for my spiritual awakening from working these steps, I share my experience with others, while practicing these principles myself, one day at a time.

Prologue

LISTEN carefully, my child, to my instructions, and attend to them with the ear of your heart. This is advice from one who loves you. Welcome it and faithfully put it into practice. The labor of obedience will bring you back to God from whom you had drifted through the sloth of disobedience.

This message of mine is for you, then, if you are ready to give up your own will, once and for all, and armed with the strong and noble weapons of obedience to do battle for Jesus, the Christ.

First of all, every time you begin a good work, you must pray to God most earnestly to bring it to perfection. In God's goodness, we are already counted as God's own, and therefore we should never grieve the Holy One by our evil actions. With the good gifts which are in us, we must obey God at all times that God may never become the angry parent who disinherits us, nor the dreaded one, enraged by our sins, who punishes us forever as worthless servants for refusing to follow the way to glory.

Lord, I begin a new work today. It is one more chance you have given me to begin again. What a blessing to have a God who forgives, who again and again invites me to start over, to tear up the messy pages of my life and start writing on a fresh pad of paper. By my *labor of obedience*, I want to return to you from whom I departed so long ago through the sloth of my own disobedience, by careless and inattentive living. I want to be attentive to you, to start listening to you right now. I've tried it the other way, listening to myself, and that has gotten me exactly nowhere, perhaps worse than nowhere—it's gotten me into big trouble.

I am ready right now for your paternal counsel. I'm ready to listen. I need to listen, and listen deeply, which literally means *to obey*.

I desperately need to renounce my own misguided will and embrace yours. I have come to the end of my rope trying to go it alone: *I admit I am powerless over my dependencies and that my life has gone out of control.*

To begin this journey, I first need to be willing to listen. Please open my ears and keep them open, Lord. Unstop them, just as you did for that deaf person when you said the word, *Ephphata*: "Be opened." Open my ears, Lord, so I may hear your loving, accepting, and welcoming voice. Amen.

January 2, May 3, September 2

Prologue (continued)

> Let us get up then, at long last, for the Scriptures rouse us when they say: "It is high time for us to arise from sleep" (Rom. 13:11). Let us open our eyes to the light that comes from God, and our ears to the voice from the heavens that every day calls out this charge: "If you hear God's voice today, do not harden your hearts" (Ps. 95:8). And again, "You that have ears to hear, listen to what the Spirit says to the churches" (Rev. 2:7). And what does the Spirit say? "Come and listen to me; I will teach you to reverence God" (Ps. 34:12). "Run while you have the light of life, that the darkness of death may not overtake you" (John 12:35).

Now is definitely the hour, Lord. It's way more than high time. I've been asleep for how long? That fantasy world of addiction is a world of make believe, a world of phony dreams and noxious nightmares. I thought that slumber was a great escape, but it proved to be a never-never land, a land of dreams that would never satisfy, of promises that could never be kept. Yes, it's time for me to wake up and to get on with real life in real time. That would be your time, Lord, the blessed reality of every ticking second.

I know. I have to run, and run fast, while I still have the light of life lest the darkness completely overtake me. Those words couldn't ring truer in my soul. I have already lived under the darkness of death. It has overtaken me more than once. The darkness always seemed to have won. It always seemed to get the best of me, because I wouldn't listen for your voice. Instead, I listened to the selfish voices in my own head. I didn't look for it and therefore I couldn't see *the light that comes from God*. Someone else called it your *deifying light*. How I love that expression. That's the kind of light that can reshape me into your image and likeness, just like you created me.

If today I hear your voice. Lord, if in the next twenty-four hours you should beckon to me, please let me hear you clearly. Help me shut out all those competing voices *that would corrupt and destroy the creatures of God*, voices that would distract me from focusing on you and you alone. At least for these next twenty-four hours I'm counting on you to protect me, Lord. Amen.

January 3, May 4, September 3

Prologue (continued)

> Seeking workers in a multitude of people, God calls out and says again: "Is there anyone here who yearns for life and desires to see good days?" (Ps. 34:13). If you hear this and your answer is "I do," God then directs these words to you: If you desire true and eternal life, "keep your tongue free from vicious talk and your lips from all deceit; turn away from evil and do good; let peace be your quest and aim" (Ps. 34:14–15). Once you have done this, my "eyes will be upon you and my ears will listen for your prayers; and even before you ask me, I will say to you: "Here I am" (Isa. 58:9). What is more delightful than this voice of the Holy One calling to us? See how God's love shows us the way of life. Clothed then with faith and the performance of good works, let us set out on this way, with the Gospel for our guide, that we may deserve to see the Holy One "who has called us to the eternal presence" (1 Thess. 2:12).

Is there anyone here who yearns for life and desires to see good days? What a question. Who wouldn't? Yet, by giving in to my unhealthy appetites I have chosen the opposite of life: death itself.

In the heat of the moment I have often failed to *[keep] my tongue free of vicious talk [and] my lips from all deceit.* I have lied plenty to cover up my hidden life and mask my shadow side. And in the throes of my compulsions I have viciously attacked people who dared even mildly to disagree with me. I was a constant critic with nothing constructive to offer. My resentments abounded. Perceived offenses, even slight ones, I met with open hostility. "Don't cross me," I'd think; "I'll get you for it later."

What a nasty way to live. What a perfect path toward spiritual death.

"Turn away from evil and do good; let peace be your quest and aim." I found it hard to do that. It was easier to be nasty, critical, cynical, and caustic about others rather than to be positive and affirming. I took the proverbial path of least resistance: don't just get angry, get even.

Yet now I seek the serenity of recovery: that "peace . . . which surpasses all understanding" (Phil. 4:7). Said Jesus, "Peace I leave with you; my peace I give to you. I do not give to you as the world gives. Do not let your hearts be troubled, and do not let them be afraid" (John 14:27). I need that kind of peace.

God promises to be there with me, even when I am just trying to seek his kind of peace—trying to build positive relationships with my fellow human beings. In that moment, God speaks words of love and affirmation to me in that delightful voice of his. God whispers in my ear: "You don't need that anymore. Let me show you a more excellent way" (1 Cor. 12:31, adapted).

January 4, May 5, September 4

Prologue (continued)

If we wish to dwell in God's tent, we will never arrive unless we run there by doing good deeds. But let us ask with the Prophet, "Who will dwell in Your tent, O God; who will find rest upon Your holy mountain?" (Ps. 15:1).

After this question, then, let us listen well to what God says in reply, for we are shown the way to God's tent. "Those who walk without blemish and are just in all dealings; who speak truth from the heart and have not practiced deceit; who have not wronged another in any way, not listened to slander against a neighbor" (Ps. 15:2–3).

They have foiled the evil one at every turn (Ps. 15:4), flinging both the devil and these wicked promptings far from sight. While these temptations were still "young, the just caught hold of them and dashed them against Christ" (Ps. 15:4, 137:9).

These people reverence God, and do not become elated over their own good deeds; they judge it is God's strength, not their own, that brings about the good in them. "They praise" (Ps. 15:4), the Holy One working in them, and say with the prophet: "Not to us, O God, not to us give the glory, but to your name alone" (Ps. 115:1). In just this way, Paul the apostle refused to take credit for the power of his preaching. He declared: "By God's grace I am what I am" (1 Cor. 15:10). And again Paul said: "Those who boast should make their boast in God" (2 Cor. 10:17).

Dwelling under the protective shelter of God's tent is difficult to do unless I do something good for someone other than myself. The twelfth step is the "pass-it-on" step: *Grateful for spiritual awakening from walking these steps, I share my experience with others, while practicing these principles myself, one day at a time.* In my morning meditation, I am asked to pray for the person who is still sick, for my recovering sister or brother still struggling with the pull of addiction. But besides praying, I need to share my pilgrimage, for better or for worse, with another human being. Meetings are a precious opportunity to share deeply one's sorrows and joys, one's successes and failures *as we trudge the Road of Happy Destiny.*

And here's a practical tip about temptation I can't afford to miss: *While these temptations are still young, I catch hold of them and dash them against Christ.* In other words, surrender early: get out while the getting is good.

Lord, in the past, I have dallied a bit too long, played with fire and got burnt, sometimes badly. Now, more and more I feel led to turn away quicker. Dash that thought against the Rock of Ages. It won't hurt the rock but it could hurt *me* badly. If I hang onto that thought, it will get me hooked again sooner or later, and the struggle to recover my lost sobriety will begin all over again.

At least for the next twenty-four hours, let me visualize you, Lord, as my Rock, hard as diamond, the sturdiest stone of all. Let me shatter temptation against you before temptation shatters me. Lord, I claim you as my tent and shelter, my rock and refuge. Amen.

January 5, May 6, September 5

Prologue (continued)

> That is why it is said in the Gospel: "Whoever hears these words of mine and does them, is like a wise person who built a house upon rock; the floods came and the winds blew and beat against the house, but it did not fall: it was founded on rock" (Matt. 7:24–25).
>
> With this conclusion, God waits for us daily to translate into action, as we should, these holy teachings. Therefore, our lifespan has been lengthened by way of a truce, that we may amend our misdeeds. As the apostle says: "Do you not know that the patience of God is leading you to repent?" (Rom. 2:4). And God indeed assures us in love: "I do not wish the death of sinners, but that they turn back to me and live" (Ezek. 33:11).

The house on the rock. I can see it now: a beautiful summer home built by the sea. A gorgeous beach, an infinite expanse of water, the sound of seagulls, the sensation of wind across my face—everywhere your presence, Lord, in the still serenity of an ocean vista.

But living by the sea can be both beautiful and treacherous. Storms can arise, and they will. Big waves and powerful winds may prevail. That's the price I must pay for such a beautiful environment. You tell me it'll be okay if I remember to build my seaside home on your bedrock, rather than on the shifting sands of my own emotions. I know I need to do just that. No matter what may come, I can both enjoy the beauty and weather the storms.

My unruly appetites may flare up at any given moment: all addiction is *baffling, cunning, and powerful.* Yet, with your Rock still in sight, I have a living reminder that you are there, Lord. The storms of human passion may brew, the winds of self-gratification may threaten, but if for even a split second I can remember the Rock, perhaps I can escape ruin and peril, one more time.

Lord, daily you wait for me to translate all this theory into practice. *Twenty-four hours* are my saving watchwords. On a daily basis, you promise always to be there for me, as I try to put your teachings into action.

Unfortunately, it's a trial and error process; I wish it weren't. I wish you would just snap your fingers and it would be ever and always so. But your humanity, Lord, empathizes with my weakness, and you are patient. So patient, in fact, that you lengthen my life just to give me more time to try and get it right. What a Lord, what a God you are. One who encourages rather than one who chastises.

Truly, the infinite patience of a loving God leads me to repent. Though my efforts must always be finite, I thank you in victory, as well as in defeat, for you remain a God of mercy, kindness, and love. Amen.

January 6, May 7, September 6

Prologue (continued)

Now that we have asked God who will dwell in the holy tent, we have heard the instruction for dwelling in it, but only if we fulfill the obligations of those who live there. We must, then, prepare our hearts and bodies for the battle of holy obedience to God's instructions. What is not possible to us by nature, let us ask the Holy One to supply by the help of grace. If we wish to reach eternal life, even as we avoid the torments of hell, then—while there is still time, while we are in this body and have time to accomplish all these things by the light of life—we must run and do now what will profit us forever.

What doesn't come to us naturally, let us ask the Holy One to supply by the help of grace. Or to say that as a prayer: *That you, O God, may be pleased to give me the help of your grace for anything that my weak human nature finds hardly possible.* If that doesn't hit the nail on the head for me, Lord. Temptation has so many different pathways to get at me. How that happens continues to *baffle, outwit, and overpower.*

I want to dwell in *your* tent, Lord, and fulfill all the duties and obligations you have for me, but I can't do that by myself. I cannot wage that level of battle single-handedly; I need you there at my side: to my left, to my right, in front of me, behind me, above me and beneath me, as prayed in the hymn attributed to St. Patrick ("St. Patrick's Breastplate," #370, *Hymnal 1982*).

For sure, this is the *battle of holy obedience*. To fight this one simply by relying on my human nature, my human willpower, is to fight a losing battle. To do battle infused by your overflowing grace at least makes victory possible. The *light of life*, dear Lord, is key for me here, lest I stray back into the shadows, into the *valley of the shadow of death* (Ps. 23).

Yes, Lord. I must hasten to do right now what will profit me for all eternity: to address the *baffling, cunning, and powerful* nature of my addiction outfitted with no less than your full armor (Eph. 6:13–17). "Yours, O Lord, is the greatness, the power, the glory, the victory, and the majesty; for all that is in the heavens and on the earth is yours; yours is the kingdom, O Lord, and you are exalted as head above all" (1 Chron. 29:11). Amen.

January 7, May 8, September 7

Prologue (concluded)

> Therefore, we intend to establish a school for God's service. In drawing up its regulations, we hope to set down nothing harsh, nothing burdensome. The good of all concerned, however, may prompt us to a little strictness in order to amend faults and to safeguard love. Do not be daunted immediately by fear and run away from the road that leads to salvation. It is bound to be narrow at the outset (Matt. 7:14). But as we progress in this way of life and in faith, we shall run on the path of God's commandments, our hearts overflowing with the inexpressible delight of love (Ps. 119:32). Never swerving from God's instructions, then, but faithfully observing God's teaching in the monastery until death, we shall through patience share in the sufferings of Christ (1 Pet. 4:13) that we may deserve also to share in the eternal presence. Amen.

Lord, these words remind me that I must consciously observe a certain strictness of lifestyle in order to amend my faults and safeguard genuine love. I no longer want that counterfeit kind of self-absorbed love that led me down unwholesome paths in the first place. If *I am fully prepared for you to remove all my character defects*, then I must do my part and be serious about amendment of life. Especially at the outset of my journey, I need to tread the narrow path of self-discipline that prepares me for sober living.

My *path to recovery* need neither be *harsh nor burdensome.* It could be delightful and rewarding. For it to be so, I must aspire to a stricter code of sobriety, beginning with a practice known as "custody of the eyes."

The eye has been called the window of the soul. As such, in this *school of the Lord's service,* I need to keep my windows clean and my eyes trained on my Higher Power. Beginning this journey, Lord, I am fully prepared for you to outfit me with an appropriate pair of "blinders." Blinders are there literally to keep horses on track. Put those blinders on me, Lord, and keep me on track.

As I daily struggle toward spiritual integrity, may the heart you have given me expand to be filled with the sweetness of your love. Amen.

January 8, May 9, September 8

CHAPTER 1: The Kinds of Monks

There are clearly four kinds of monastics. First, there are the *cenobites,* that is to say, those who belong to a monastery, where they serve under a rule and an abbot or prioress.

Second, there are the *anchorites* or hermits who have come through the test of living in a monastery for a long time and have passed beyond the first fervor of monastic life. Thanks to the help and guidance of many, they are now trained to fight against evil. They have built up their strength and go from the battle line in the ranks of their members to the single combat of the desert. Self-reliant now, without the support of another, they are ready with God's help to grapple single-handedly with the vices of body and mind.

Third, there are *sarabites,* the most detestable kind of monastics, who with no experience to guide them, no rule to try them as "gold is tried in a furnace" (Prov. 27:21), have a character as soft as lead. Still loyal to the world by their actions, they clearly lie to God by their signs of religion. Two or three together, or even alone, without a shepherd, they pen themselves up in their own sheepfolds, not God's. Their law is what they like to do, whatever strikes their fancy. Anything they believe in and choose, they call holy; anything they dislike, they consider forbidden.

Fourth and finally, there are the monastics called *gyrovagues*, who spend their entire lives drifting from region to region, staying as guests for three or four days in different monasteries. Always on the move, they never settle down, and are slaves to their own wills and gross appetites. In every way they are worse than sarabites.

It is better to keep silent than to speak of all these and their disgraceful way of life. Let us pass them by, then, and with the help of God, proceed to draw up a plan for the strong kind, the *cenobites*.

Lord, this section may be about different kinds of monks, but it might just as well have been written about me. I want to be like the cenobite, strongly related to my recovery community, and accountable to it. With your help, Lord, and theirs, I want to ward off the vices of the flesh and my own evil thought patterns.

But too often, Lord, I have behaved more like a sarabite, living neither under a *Rule* nor the discipline of accountability. I would go from one compulsive self-gratification to the next, whatever popped into my mind or appealed to me, whatever might strike my fancy, I was there. I was hooked. Whatever might get in my way, might call me back to sanity, I rejected and disdained. Unfortunately, I had it all backwards.

And too often, like a gyrovague, I was restlessly on the move. Adrift, I would *tramp from one place to the next, with no stability, indulging my own will and succumbing to whatever allurement of sinful pleasure next presented itself.* Like a gyrovague, I had become a slave to my own warped will and unhealthy appetites.

To observe the foibles of these various kinds of monks, I need only put a mirror to my own face, to look into my own soul. That's me there, too, monk or not.

Thomas Merton's book title, *No Man Is an Island*, comes to mind. For recovery to work for me, I know I need to be in close community and honestly accountable to my fellow travelers. *I admit to my Higher Power, to myself, and to someone else exactly what I've been doing wrong.* I need to bond strongly with my group meeting. Truly, *I have learned by the help of many brothers and sisters, how to fight against the devil.* I cannot tempt you, Lord, nor presume on you to bail me out when I have been careless about my lifestyle and have tried to go it alone.

Help me, Lord, to pattern my life after faithful monastics, lest my *baffling, cunning, and powerful* addiction overcome me and shut out your grace. Amen.

January 9, May 10, September 9

CHAPTER 2: Qualities of the Abbot or Prioress

To be worthy of the task of governing a monastery, the prioress or abbot must always remember what the title signifies and act accordingly. They are believed to hold the place of Christ in the monastery. Therefore, a prioress or abbot must never teach or decree or command anything that would deviate from God's instructions. On the contrary, everything they teach and command should, like the leaven of divine justice, permeate the minds of the community.

These words help me reflect on authority and the proper or improper use of it. Most of us, at one time or another, bear some measure of authority—maybe not the heavy-duty authority of a religious superior or a CEO, but just some kind of position where someone else reports to us. One way or another, in the workplace I may hold some measure of power over someone else, be it major or minor.

But how do I use my authority? Like a prioress or abbot, am I conscious that I exercise only *delegated* authority? Am I aware that all authority is subject to some Higher Power, some higher authority from whom it derives?

The word *authority* is based on the word *author*. It implies the originator, the owner, the initiator. God did all of that for me. If I hold any kind of authority at all, it has just been delegated to me for a certain time; it will never be mine alone, nor may I selfishly abuse it.

Have I ever, or am I now currently abusing my authority over others? In my addiction, have I ever or am I now currently using people to satisfy my own inordinate drives or insatiable appetites?

Lord, help me exercise whatever authority I may hold so as to glorify you, rather than myself. *Non nobis, Domine, non nobis, sed nomini tuo da gloriam.* Help me, like John the Baptist, to point toward you rather than toward myself. Make me think about others' needs before my own. Help me remember the Golden Rule, as I walk toward recovery and integrity. Amen.

January 10, May 11, September 10

CHAPTER 2: Qualities of the Abbot or Prioress
(continued)

Let the prioress and abbot always remember that at the judgment of God, not only their teaching but also the community's obedience will come under scrutiny. The prioress and abbot must, therefore, be aware that the shepherd will bear the blame wherever the owner of the household finds that the sheep have yielded no profit. Still, if they have faithfully shepherded a restive and disobedient flock, always striving to cure their unhealthy ways, it will be otherwise: the shepherd will be acquitted at God's judgment. Then, like the prophet, they may say to God: "I have not hidden your justice in my heart; I have proclaimed your truth and your salvation (Ps. 40:11) but they spurned and rejected me" (Isa. 1:2; Ezek. 20:27). Then at last the sheep that have rebelled against their care will be punished by the overwhelming power of death.

What is my responsibility toward other people who might be in my charge, or with whom I might be in relationship? If I have a family, what about my children? Have I taught them well? Have I equipped them with right and responsible attitudes that will help them live in the world? Have I exercised due *pastoral diligence*, carefully feeding them solid food, trying to instill right attitudes?

Often, children can be quite *unruly*, a good word in this context. *Unruly* implies adhering to no *rule*, or perhaps only sketchily or selectively so. If there has been unhealthy behavior in my family, what part might I have played in enabling that to occur? Has my own *unruly* behavior modeled a chaotic lifestyle which others have only imitated?

If teaching by example is supposed to work, how effective a teacher have I been? Have I been a wholesome model for my family, or has my behavior been deceptive and confused others? And if I am married, how has my spouse coped with my inconsistent, unpredictable ways? *But they have despised and rejected me.* The big question here might be, who has despised and who has rejected whom? *Is it I, Lord?* Has my family been so bad? Were they the ones acting out and treating me poorly? Or was it quite the reverse? Has my irresponsible behavior produced the negative responses I got?

How, Lord, can I change my behavior to foster a more wholesome environment wherever I live, whether in my family or in the larger community? *I believe in a Higher Power that can restore me to sanity,* and I trust you to heal my insanity. *Our help is in the name of the Lord, who made heaven and earth.* Amen.

January 11, May 12, September 11

CHAPTER 2: Qualities of the Abbot or Prioress
(*continued*)

Furthermore, those who receive the name of prioress or abbot are to lead the community by a twofold teaching: they must point out to the monastics all that is good and holy more by example than by words, proposing God's commandments to a receptive community with words, but demonstrating God's instructions to the stubborn and the dull by a living example. Again, if they teach the community that something is not to be done, then neither must they do it, "lest after preaching to others, they themselves be found reprobate" (1 Cor. 9:27) and God some day call to them in their sin: "How is it that you repeat my just commands and mouth my covenant when you hate discipline and toss my words behind you?" (Ps. 50:16–17). And also this: "How is it that you see a splinter in another's eye, and never notice the plank in your own?" (Matt. 7:3).

This passage, Lord, continues to keep me focused on the need to be consistent in word and deed. I find it far too easy to preach one thing and practice quite another. Not that I intend to be a hypocrite, mind you, but it just turns out that way, or so I delude myself into thinking. If the saying "practice what you preach" makes any sense whatever, what good is it for me to mouth one behavior and then do just the opposite?

The rhetorical question posed by the psalmist is really a bottom-line issue for me, Lord. It's one I should ask myself daily. Am I doing what I say I believe? "How can you spout off a list of my commandments and mouth my covenant with your lips, when in real life you just really hate discipline and toss my words in the trash?" (Ps. 49:16–17, adapted). Quite a question.

The words about *judgment* also remind me, Lord, how ready I am to criticize others, to fault them, to take offense at things they do. How easy for me to harbor resentments, get mad at people, then give myself permission to act out my addiction. "You were looking at the speck in your brother's or sister's eye and were unable to see the beam in your own" (Matt. 7:3, adapted). The splinter versus the plank once more. But step six says that *I am fully prepared for my Higher Power to remove all my character defects*, and step seven, that *I humbly ask my Higher Power to remove all my character defects*.

How blind, how oblivious have I been toward my own character defects, all the while honing my ability to pick out flaw after flaw in my neighbor. I was unable to see my own shortcomings because I was way too busy looking to project them on others.

Might all this not just be another variation of *custody of the eyes*? Where do I direct my gaze most of the time? And how badly do I need to shift that focus, for the sake of my own recovery?

January 12, May 13, September 12

CHAPTER 2: Qualities of the Abbot or Prioress
(continued)

The prioress or abbot should avoid all favoritism in the monastery. They are not to love one more than another unless they find someone better in good works and obedience. One born free is not to be given higher rank than one born a slave who becomes a monastic, except for some other good reason. But the prioress and abbot are free, if they see fit, to change anyone's rank as justice demands. Ordinarily, all are to keep to their regular places, because "whether slave or free, we are all one in Christ" (Gal. 3:28; Eph. 6:8) and share equally in the service of the one God, for "God shows no partiality among persons" (Rom. 2:11). Only in this are we distinguished in God's sight: if we are found better than others in good works and in humility. Therefore, the prioress and abbot are to show equal love to everyone and apply the same discipline to all according to their merits.

As I review my life, Lord, and my struggle for sobriety, I am keenly aware that I have often shown partiality, played favorites. I did so in my family and where I worked; I discriminated and was biased. It is still hard for me to be even-handed and fair-minded with other people. The snob inside me wants to associate only "with my own kind," or at least with those I classify as such.

Why can I still not get it, that people are people, regardless of how I might look upon them? Is this not more of the same difficulty I expressed in my last meditation? Looking upon others and judging harshly (even judging at all), instead of taking a good, long, deep look inside my own soul?

Snobbishness is a real temptation for me. I may say it's the "good chemistry" I have with so-and-so, but in reality, isn't that just another excuse to play favorites? Why do I sometimes dismiss people right off the bat, if they don't look, talk, or dress like me? I often don't even give myself a chance to establish rapport with someone new.

I wonder what it would be like if I were blind or deaf or otherwise physically impaired, so I couldn't identify how people talked or dressed?

Benedict provides some disclaimers for religious superiors regarding favoritism, although he strongly discourages the practice. For me, I see no legitimate disclaimers, no exceptions to this rule. The basics are: "God shows no partiality" (Rom 2:11; see also Peter's "aha" moment in Acts 10:34). Regardless of worldly status or title, "in Christ we are all the same, we are all on equal footing" (Gal 3:28; Eph 6:8, adapted).

Lord, having now named my vicious habit of picking and choosing whom I will love and whom I will ignore, may I ask you a favor? Let me be open to everyone, like you were down here on earth. Let me love people I would have formerly dismissed without a second thought. Grant me that moment's grace to look for your presence within them, as I search for your presence within myself. Amen.

January 13, May 14, September 13

CHAPTER 2: Qualities of the Abbot or Prioress
(continued)

In their teachings, the prioress or abbot should always observe the apostle's recommendation in which it is said: "Use argument, appeal, reproof" (2 Tim. 4:2). This means that they must vary with circumstances, threatening and coaxing by turns, at times stern, at times devoted and tender. With the undisciplined and restless, they will use firm argument; with the obedient and docile and patient, they will appeal for greater virtue; but as for the negligent and disdainful, we charge the abbot or prioress to use reproof and rebuke. They should not gloss over the sins of those who err, but cut them out while they can, as soon as they begin to sprout, remembering the fate of Eli, priest of Shiloh (1 Sam. 2:11–4:18). For the upright and perceptive, the first and second warnings should be verbal; but those who are evil or stubborn, arrogant or disobedient, can be curbed only by blows or some other physical punishment at the first offense. It is written, "The fool cannot be corrected with words" (Prov. 29:19), and again, "Strike your children with a rod and you will free their souls from death" (Prov. 23:14).

As a professor, I tried to convince my teaching assistants that one size does not fit all. For a time, the buzzword in education was "individualized instruction." Teachers customized the learning package to fit the individual learner's style. Like most teaching fads, individualized instruction came and went. Yet the basic principle was solid: a single, lockstep teaching method does not work for everyone. An eclectic method utilizing various techniques generally works better.

Such thinking seems useful to me now on my pilgrimage toward healing. At different stages of life, different spiritual strategies work better than others. My spiritual life is an evolving, rather than a static adventure. I need to adapt, be flexible, and open myself to new prayer forms.

While this part of the *Rule* discusses how the superior is to apply discipline to his or her charges, I can apply such self-discipline to my own spiritual life. At times, I too am quite *undisciplined and restless,* at other times *obedient, docile, and patient.* Sometimes I am *negligent and disdainful,* sometimes *upright and perceptive.* I cannot always be the same steady believer I'd like to be. For me, one size never seems to fit all. I must constantly adapt and revise my spiritual routine. I must be a wise eclectic. Yet from what psychology teaches us today, we know that "blows or some other physical punishment" or to "strike your children with a rod" frees no one's soul from anything. To be cruel to oneself or to another rather wreaks only more havoc in a restless spirit.

The doctor who self-treats, it has been said, has a fool for a patient. Therefore, I am happy to have a spiritual director I can go to for regular checkups. Lord, I do want to recover, and realize that this is a lifelong pursuit. Thank you for various spiritual disciplines that can help me toward my goal. Amen.

January 14, May 15, September 14

CHAPTER 2: Qualities of the Abbot or Prioress
(continued)

The prioress or abbot must always remember what they are and what they are called, aware that more will be expected of one to whom more has been entrusted. They must know what a difficult and demanding burden they have undertaken: directing souls and serving a variety of temperaments, coaxing, reproving, and encouraging them as appropriate. They must so accommodate and adapt themselves to each one's character and intelligence that they will not only keep the flock entrusted to their care from dwindling but will rejoice in the increase of a good flock.

Lord, I know only too well the spiritual principle, that *more will be expected of one to whom more has been entrusted* (Luke 12:48). And I am painfully aware of the many gifts and graces you have given me, and that my burden is to make something of them. But for many years I have squandered those assets, wasting time and resources I can never recover. Yet I can do something about today: *take courage to change the things I can*, at least for twenty-four hours.

Once more it becomes clear to me: I, too, *must adjust and adapt* to situations as they arise. If I try to deal with every temptation the same way, I will more than likely fail. Let me become like supple, moist clay, Lord, in your Potter's hands, so that you may remold me in your own image and likeness.

Nor let me dwell on past, missed opportunities or squandered resources. Instead, let me thank you for this present moment where I now *live and move and have my being*, where right now I can embrace your living, loving presence. Amen.

January 15, May 16, September 15

CHAPTER 2: Qualities of the Abbot or Prioress
(concluded)

Above all, they must not show too great a concern for the fleeting and temporal things of this world, neglecting or treating lightly the welfare of those entrusted to them. Rather, they should keep in mind that they have undertaken the care of souls for whom they must give an account. That they may not plead lack of resources as an excuse, they are to remember what is written: "Seek first the reign and justice of God, and all these things will be given to you as well" (Matt. 6:33), and again, "Those who reverence the Holy One lack nothing" (Ps. 34:10). The prioress and abbot must know that anyone undertaking the charge of souls must be ready to account for them. Whatever the number of members they have in their care, let them realize that on judgment day they will surely have to submit a reckoning to God for all their souls—and indeed for their own as well. In this way, while always fearful of the future examination of the shepherds about the sheep entrusted to them and careful about the state of others' accounts, they become concerned also about their own, and while helping others to amend by their warnings, they achieve the amendment of their own faults.

This passage helps me put life into perspective. It is so easy to get caught up in *the temporal, the fleeting, the perishable things of this world* that I wind up undervaluing the welfare of my soul.

A varied, flexible, yet disciplined spiritual life will hopefully help me avoid this pitfall, Lord. If I say my prayers every morning or evening, if I think of you now and then during the day, if I rehearse the twelve steps or even focus on the "step of the month," I may avoid forgetting that which is most precious: the health and welfare of my immortal soul.

"Seek first the kingdom of God and God's justice, and all these [other temporal] things shall be given you besides" (Matt. 6:33, adapted). First things first: how simple. Nothing must be allowed to displace my spiritual life. But it can't begin and end there. The twelfth step calls for sharing: *Grateful for spiritual awakening from walking these steps, I share my experience with others, while practicing these principles myself, one day at a time.*

Abbot and prioress are reminded that while helping others to amend their lives, they themselves are likewise being cleansed of their own faults. By helping another, I ultimately help myself. Whatever tiny crust of bread I toss on the waters somehow comes back a full loaf. Somehow that miracle takes place. Amen.

January 16, May 17, September 16

CHAPTER 3: Summoning the Community for Counsel

As often as anything important is to be done in the monastery, the prioress or abbot shall call the whole community together and explain what the business is; and after hearing the advice of the members, let them ponder it and follow what they judge the wiser course. The reason why we have said all should be called for counsel is that the Spirit often reveals what is better to the younger. The community members, for their part, are to express their opinions with all humility, and not presume to defend their own views obstinately. The decision is rather the prioress's or the abbot's to make, so that when the abbot or prioress of the community has determined what is more prudent, all must obey. Nevertheless, just as it is proper for disciples to obey their teacher, so it is becoming for the teacher to settle everything with foresight and fairness.

Taking counsel with others, especially my fellow travelers in recovery, I find both essential and rewarding. As the superior is called to consult with the community yet must personally make the final decision, so I too am smart to listen to the opinions of those with whom I journey. It is I who still must take personal responsibility for my own recovery work.

I also find it true that younger sojourners often show great insight into the process of recovery. And, as the *Rule* prescribes, and as we practice in our meetings, people *offer their advice humbly*. We do not *presume stubbornly to defend our own opinions*, but just offer our experience, for better or for worse.

For me, meetings are always *important business*, and places of grace and energy, reflecting the synergy of the group. How often after a meeting have we remarked, "Powerful meeting!" That happens when each of us speaks in the "I" and witnesses to our personal pilgrimage, *trudging the Road of Happy Destiny*.

Two heads—preferably even more—are better than one. And *wherever two or three are gathered together* somehow our Higher Power is there too. For me, meetings seem to be where the Way, the Truth, and the Life converge and energize.

January 17, May 18, September 17

CHAPTER 3: Summoning the Community for Counsel (concluded)

Accordingly, in every instance, all are to follow the teaching of the rule, and no one shall rashly deviate from it. In the monastery, monastics are not to follow their own heart's desire, nor shall they presume to contend with the prioress or abbot defiantly, or outside the monastery. Should any presume to do so, let them be subjected to the discipline of the rule.

Moreover, the prioress or abbot must personally reverence God and keep the rule in everything they do; they can be sure beyond any doubt that they will have to give an account of all their judgments to God, the most just of judges.

If less important business of the monastery is to be transacted, the prioress and abbot shall take counsel with the elders only, as it is written: "Do everything with counsel and you will not be sorry afterward" (Sir. 32:24).

To undergo the discipline of the rule. To be subject to the discipline of the rule. In all things, therefore, let all follow the rule as guide, and let no one be so rash as to deviate from it.

These insights concluding the chapter on counsel in the community are important because they remind me of the necessity of having a personal *Rule of Life*. Whether I write one down or not, I have one: a transcript of my daily lifestyle, a record of what I do and what I don't do.

For the Benedictine, following the *Rule* is the basis for behavior. My Benedictine heart needs a *Rule,* and I need to follow it. Just to float or catch-as-catch-can in spiritual life will get me nowhere, or worse, get me somewhere I don't need to be.

I need some kind of a system to deal with life because life itself is generally quite unsystematic and surprising. My *Rule*, as simple as it might be, helps me monitor progress and assess any disparity between my intentions and my actions.

For me to go through life with no personal *Rule*, no measuring stick, is to court disaster. While having a *Rule* doesn't guarantee I will keep it perfectly, at least there are guidelines I can return to.

Thank you, Lord, for the *Rule of Benedict*. Please help me consider crafting my own personal *Rule* to order my life. Amen.

January 18, May 19, September 18

CHAPTER 4: The Tools for Good Works

First of all, "love God with your whole heart, your whole soul and all your strength, and love your neighbor as yourself" (Matt. 22:37–39; Mark 12: 30–31; Luke 10:27). Then the following: "You are not to kill, not to commit adultery; you are not to steal nor to covet" (Rom. 13:9); "you are not to bear false witness" (Matt. 19:18; Mark 10:19; Luke 18:20). "You must honor everyone" (1 Pet. 2:17), and "never do to another what you do not want done to yourself" (Tob. 4:16; Matt. 7:12; Luke 6:31). Renounce yourself in order to follow Christ (Matt. 16:24; Luke 9:23); discipline your body (1 Cor. 9:27); "do not pamper yourself, but love fasting." You must relieve the lot of the poor, "clothe the naked, visit the sick" (Matt. 25:36), and bury the dead. Go to help the troubled and console the sorrowing. Your way of acting should be different from the world's way; the love of Christ must come before all else.

How difficult to choose from among so many lofty goals for living the spiritual life.

From time to time, some goals will stand out more than others. Which ones stand out for me today? From time to time, I select various tools from the toolbox: different tools for different times, different instruments for different operations, different issues to address at different stages of life. The following seem particularly important now.

To "honor everyone" (1 Pet. 2:17) reminds me to be careful about discriminatory behavior. The reading for January 12, May 13, and September 12 (RB 2,16ff.) makes a pretty cogent case against favoritism. In preferring one person over another, I dishonor the one I marginalize. Do I tend to judge people by external criteria: how they look, how they talk, dress, whether they impress me or not? Is this fair? Is this Christian? Is this Benedictine? I would be embarrassed to answer these questions honestly.

Then the goal *to renounce or deny oneself in order to follow Christ*—that's a toughie for me. I never much liked the idea of self-denial. It's not my style. I much prefer luxury and comfort, with all the bells, whistles, and perks of the "good" life: five-star hotels rather than camping grounds.

I seldom reflect that by hogging and hoarding all that for myself, I might be depriving someone else of having even a moderately good life. Is such inequity right? Could I not get by on less, much less, so that others might have at least something? I know I need to try.

The last goal here warns me *not to become attached to pleasures*. This sounds like more of the same. If I *pamper myself* with all life's accessories, am I not attaching myself to *things that are transitory, rather than things that will endure?* Isn't that going in the wrong direction? I don't just *think* so; I *know* so. I know better. Lord, please help straighten me out. I desperately need *to become (more of) a stranger to the world's ways,* and less of a stranger to yours. Amen.

January 19, May 20, September 19

CHAPTER 4: The Tools for Good Works (continued)

> You are not to act in anger or nurse a grudge. Rid your heart of all deceit. Never give a hollow greeting of peace or turn away when someone needs your love. Bind yourselves to no oath lest it prove false but speak the truth with heart and tongue. "Do not repay one bad turn with another" (1 Thess. 5:15; 1 Pet. 3:9). Do not injure anyone but bear injuries patiently. "Love your enemies" (Matt. 5:44; Luke 6:27). If people curse you, do not curse them back but bless them instead. "Endure persecution for the sake of justice" (Matt. 5:10). "You must not be proud, nor be given to wine" (Titus 1:7; 1 Tim.3:3). Refrain from too much eating or sleeping, and "from laziness" (Rom. 12:11). Do not grumble or speak ill of others. Place your hope in God alone. If you notice something good in yourself, give credit to God, not to yourself, but be certain that the evil you commit is always your own and yours to acknowledge.

It is interesting that the first part of this passage concentrates on relapse triggers and then lists various addictions. Giving way to anger, nursing grudges, or harboring resentments are all typical reasons for me to start self-medicating again.

When these feelings start, I know it's time for an attitude adjustment. How often am I tempted to *forsake charity, to want to return evil for evil,* to get even with someone whom I consider offensive? How easy it is to curse someone who has done me wrong. Full of pride, I am anything but patient with anyone I see as the enemy.

Warped attitudes like these need to be nailed promptly, or before I know it I will be back to acting out, self-medicating perceived wounds. And then addictive behaviors are likely to follow: whether overeating, overspending, lusting, binging, gambling, being slothful, or just plain wasting time. Whatever my drug of choice, I will take whatever dose may be required to dull my pain, as my addictive cycle resumes.

Healing words come toward the end of this passage. First and foremost, I must put my hope in God, I must *believe in a Higher Power that can restore me to sanity* (step two). I must attribute to God whatever good I see in myself, or what may have come from sticking with the program. And finally, I need to admit to myself that whatever evil I allow to reenter my life is my responsibility—no one else's. I can lay it at no other doorstep than my own.

January 20, May 21, September 20

CHAPTER 4: The Tools for Good Works (continued)

Live in fear of Judgment Day and have a great horror of hell. Yearn for everlasting life with holy desire. Day by day remind yourself that you are going to die. Hour by hour keep careful watch over all you do, aware that God's gaze is upon you, wherever you may be. As soon as wrongful thoughts come into your heart, dash them against Christ and disclose them to your spiritual guide. Guard your lips from harmful or deceitful speech. Prefer moderation in speech and speak no foolish chatter, nothing to provoke laughter; do not love immoderate or boisterous laughter. Listen readily to holy reading and devote yourself often to prayer. Every day with tears and sighs, confess your past sins to God in prayer and change from these evil ways in the future. "Do not gratify the promptings of the flesh" (Gal. 5:16); hate the urgings of self-will. Obey the orders of the prioress and abbot unreservedly, even if their own conduct—which God forbid—be at odds with what they say. Remember the teachings of the Holy One: "Do what they say, not what they do" (Matt. 23:3). Do not aspire to be called holy before you really are, but first be holy that you may more truly be called so.

The most important thing for me today is *to desire eternal life with all the passion of the spirit*. If I can truly want this with all my heart and soul and mind, then I must order my life accordingly. Eternal life doesn't begin after death; it begins now. You, Lord, are in the here and now. That's where God is to be found, not later on or somewhere else, but within me, right now.

If this passionate desire for the life of the Spirit is to be alive in me now, and to stay for good, I need *to keep constant guard over the actions of my life*. I cannot let down my guard, whether that means *guarding my tongue against evil and depraved speech* or guarding against the kind of thinking that produces such speech.

The *Rule* de-emphasizes verbiage and verbosity. It cautions us about what we say and how we use our voices: *not to love much talking; not to speak useless words or words that move to laughter; not to love much or boisterous laughter*. I would do well to say less, to avoid idle chatter, to reflect more, be less the comedian, less the joker. Benedict sees much of the world's idle chatter for what it is: "whistling in the dark" as we try to fill the lacunae of life with silliness rather than substance.

Whenever I try to play the clown or whenever I laugh out loud, am I often not just trying to drown out my own sadness? Are these not precious yet wasted moments? I can't connect with you, Lord, for my own rowdiness. Please help me come to quiet, help me listen and hear what you want to tell me. Help me stop drowning you out with inane chatter. Life is too short to waste it on absurdity. Amen.

January 21, May 22, September 21

CHAPTER 4: The Tools for Good Works (concluded)

Live by God's commandments every day; treasure chastity, harbor neither hatred nor jealously of anyone, and do nothing out of envy. Do not love quarreling; shun arrogance. Respect the elders and love the young. Pray for your enemies out of love for Christ. If you have a dispute with someone, make peace with that person before the sun goes down. These then are the tools of the spiritual craft. When we have used them without ceasing day and night and have returned them on the day of judgment, our wages will be the reward God has promised: "What the eye has not seen nor the ear heard, God has prepared for those who love"

(1 Cor. 2:9). The workshop where we are to toil faithfully at all these tasks is the enclosure of the monastery and stability in the community.

The first task in this last series is perhaps the most important: *to fulfill God's commandments daily in one's deeds*. It is the daily living out of the spiritual life that makes sense, the knitting together of one present moment to the next, in which I have God and God's rules in front of me.

The concluding section again reminds me about the need to exclude all negativity from my thoughts and actions: hating no one, not being jealous or envious, neither contentious, haughty, nor disrespectful.

These *tools of the spiritual craft*, these instruments at my disposal, are given to me for a season; they are simply on loan and are expected to be returned when my earthly journey is complete. If I use them to build a life, and use them well, you will be pleased, Lord, and I hope, someday will welcome me home. But I need to work with these tools on a daily basis. I need to make sure none are neglected or go missing from my toolbox. I need to take proper care of each tool and one day return them all in good condition.

For the full-time monastic, the monastery enclosure is where all this happens. It is there that the monk or nun promises to stay and work. As an oblate or part-time monastic, someone living out in the world, I owe a similar pledge of *stability to the community* where I live. I need to be a good citizen, a good employee, and a good human being. I am grateful, Lord, for the many tools of good works you have given me to help me be more loyal, present, and caring to those around me. Amen.

January 22, May 23, September 22

CHAPTER 5: Obedience

The first step of humility is unhesitating obedience, which comes naturally to those who cherish Christ above all. Because of the holy service they have professed, or because of dread of hell and for the glory of everlasting life, they carry out the orders of the prioress or abbot as promptly as if the command came directly from God. The Holy One says of people like this: "No sooner did they hear than they obeyed me"

(Ps. 18:45); again, God tells teachers: "Whoever listens to you, listens to me" (Luke 10:16). Such people as these immediately put aside their own concerns, abandon their own will, and lay down whatever they have in hand, leaving it unfinished. With the ready step of obedience, they follow the voice of authority in their actions. Almost at the same moment, then, as the teacher gives the instruction the disciple quickly puts it into practice out of reverence for God; and both actions together are swiftly completed as one. It is love that impels them to pursue everlasting life; therefore, they are eager to take the narrow road of which God says: "Narrow is the road that leads to life (Matt. 7:14). They no longer live by their own judgment, giving in to their whims and appetites; rather they walk according to another's decisions and directions, choosing to live in monasteries and to have a prioress or abbot over them. Monastics of this resolve unquestionably conform to the saying of Christ: "I have come not to do my own will, but the will of the One who sent me" (John 6:38).

Obedience, or *deep listening* in its most literal meaning, is generally unpopular. Contemporary culture tells me I am the master of my own destiny, a rugged individualist accountable to no one but myself.

This introductory section on obedience, however, tells me that *such as these*, meaning people committed to working daily on their spiritual life, are committed *therefore, immediately to leave their own affairs and forsake their own will, dropping whatever they were engaged in and leaving it unfinished.*

What *I* have to forsake are my own worthless pursuits and selfish behaviors. These former activities I must now completely abandon. This includes anything or anyone related to my former addictive lifestyle. As an addict, I lived out destructive behavior patterns that needed to be broken and replaced with healthier habits. As Benedict puts it, *I must move out with the ready step of obedience so that my deeds follow the voice of God rather than my own.*

No longer may I *live according to my own misguided choices nor obey the voice of my own desires and pleasures, going by my own judgment and giving in to my every whim and appetite.* Instead, I need to change channels for good. I need to tune in to what God is trying to tell me: live healthy, seek sanity, love prudently. I trust you, Lord, to enable me to listen deeply and respond positively to your voice. There is none sweeter. Amen.

January 23, May 24, September 23

CHAPTER 5: Obedience (concluded)

> This very obedience, however, will be acceptable to God and agreeable to people only if compliance with what is commanded is not cringing or sluggish or halfhearted, but free from any grumbling or any reaction of unwillingness. For the obedience shown to an abbot or prioress is given to God, who has said: "Whoever listens to you, listens to me" (Luke 10:16). Furthermore, the disciples' obedience must be given gladly, for "God loves a cheerful giver" (2 Cor. 9:7). If disciples obey grudgingly and grumble, not only aloud but also in their hearts, then, even though the order is carried out, their actions will not be accepted with favor by God, who sees that they are grumbling in their hearts. These disciples will have no reward for service of this kind; on the contrary, they will incur punishment for grumbling, unless they change for the better and make amends.

The spirit of *how* I do something is as important as, or perhaps even more important, than *what* I do. Benedict makes a strong case against whiners and gripers, as well as against procrastinators. He says the only kind of obedience that really counts is when the assignment is done *without hesitation, delay, half-heartedness, grumbling, or objection. Disciples should offer their obedience with a good will, for "God loves a cheerful giver."* Intentionality plays a key role in spiritual life. Sin lies not so much in the act as in the intention. Virtue is more related to my attitude than to my accomplishments.

We are not sure exactly what it would be, but Benedict promises to punish those who obey grudgingly rather than cheerfully. The point I take from this, Lord, is that if you talk to me and ask me to do something, I ought to listen carefully and respond cheerfully, no matter what you ask. I should be grateful you want to talk to me in the first place. And I should respond by carrying out what you want, to the best of my ability.

Like the disciples you called along the lakeshore, let me promptly drop *my* nets—the stuff that's got me all tangled up—*without delay* and without complaining. Let me just joyfully come and follow you. Amen.

January 24, May 25, September 24

CHAPTER 6: Restraint of Speech

Let us follow the prophet's counsel: "I said, I have resolved to keep watch over my ways that I may never sin with my tongue. I was silent and was humbled, and I refrained even from good words" (Ps. 39:2–3). Here the prophet indicates that there are times when even good words are to be left unsaid out of esteem for silence. For all the more reason, then, should evil speech be curbed so that punishment for sin may be avoided. Indeed, so important is silence that permission to speak should seldom be granted even to mature disciples, no matter how good or holy or constructive their talk, because it is written: "In a flood of words you will not avoid sin" (Prov. 10:19); and elsewhere, "The tongue holds the key to life and death" (Prov. 18:21). Speaking and teaching are the teacher's task; the disciple is to be silent and listen.

Therefore, any requests to an abbot or prioress should be made with all humility and respectful submission. We absolutely condemn in all places any vulgarity and gossip and talk leading to laughter, and we do not permit a disciple to engage in words of that kind.

The world I live in is a noisy world. Much sound, little substance. One of the great appeals of monastic life is its emphasis on silence, or at least modest, reasonable conversation. Idle chatter, boisterous laughter, trivial talk is out in a Benedictine lifestyle. The emphasis is on quality in all things, including the spoken word.

The world needs constant sound, and most of it is neither sensible sound nor intelligent communication but simply noise. The term "noise pollution" comes to mind. Some municipalities even have laws about such things.

Benedict points out from scripture that the spirit of silence ought to lead me at times to refrain even from good conversation, which my world would hardly understand. If it's good, why not say it? Why not talk about good things?

Limiting my use of even legitimate conversation can help sensitize me to the dangers of unbridling the tongue for sinful speech. *I will guard my ways, lest I may sin with my tongue. I have set a guard to my mouth.* Limiting how much I talk may lessen the likelihood of drifting into negativity and eventually gossip.

How can I practice such restraint? How can I cut down useless chatter, often but the doorway to gossip and slander? My morning meditation time helps me focus on listening quietly to you, Lord, and already begins to limit the time I might otherwise waste on small talk.

This short chapter, itself one of few words, invites me to the wonder of silence. May the spirit of silence become real for me. May I come to value it more and more. Rather than seeing silence as the absence of sound, let me embrace it as the gently whispering wind of your presence, Lord, deep in my soul. Amen.

January 25, May 26, September 25

CHAPTER 7: Humility

Sisters and Brothers, divine Scripture calls to us saying: "For all who exalt themselves will be humbled, and those who humble themselves will be exalted" (Luke 14:11; 18:14). In saying this, therefore, it shows us that every exaltation is a kind of pride, which the prophet indicates has been shunned, saying: "O God, my heart is not exalted; my eyes are not lifted up and I have not walked in the ways of the great nor gone after marvels beyond me" (Ps. 131:1). And why? If I had not a humble spirit, but were exalted instead, then you would treat me like a weaned child on its mother's lap" (Ps. 131:2).

Accordingly, if we want to reach the highest summit of humility, if we desire to attain speedily that exaltation in heaven to which we climb by the humility of this present life, then by our ascending actions we must set up that ladder on which Jacob in a dream saw "angels descending and ascending" (Gen. 28:12). Without doubt, this descent and ascent can signify only that we descend by exaltation and ascend by humility. Now the ladder erected is our life on earth, and if we humble our hearts God will raise it to heaven. We may call our body and soul the sides of this ladder, into which our divine vocation has fitted the various steps of humility and discipline as we ascend.

The analogy of Jacob's ladder is surely a picturesque one. I like the sides of the ladder representing body and soul, and appreciate the inverse proportionality of what is going up and what is coming down. What is upward mobility from my world perspective? What does "climb the ladder of success" mean for me? And how does any of this relate to living life in the spirit?

Without doubt, this descent and ascent can signify only that we descend by self-exaltation and ascend by humility. I must have had it all backwards. Again, I am confronted with the gospel paradox: what *seems* to be up is down, and what *seems* to be down is up. Whoever pilots an aircraft on instruments rather than by visual reference, must rely solely on what the avionics say and not on however the pilot might perceive the aircraft's attitude, whether right side up or upside down. So too in the spiritual life: I need to trust God's gauges, especially scripture, to keep me grounded in reality rather than leave me floating in fantasy.

I'm afraid, Lord, that for too long I have ignored your instrument panel, drifting off the glide path of real life into fantasy. I didn't watch nor did I heed *your* instruments, *your* gauges. Only you, Lord, can keep me on true course, and tell me whether I am gaining or losing altitude, whether I'm ascending or descending the ladder of the spirit, whether I'm being prideful or humble. Please help me follow your sense of direction, and quit relying on my own often misguided notions. Amen.

January 26, May 27, September 26

CHAPTER 7: Humility *(continued)*

The first step of humility, then, is that we keep "the reverence of God always before our eyes" (Ps. 36:2) and never forget it. We must constantly remember everything God has commanded, keeping in mind that all who despise God will burn in hell for their sins, and all who reverence God have everlasting life awaiting them. Let us guard ourselves at every moment from sins and vices of thought or tongue, of hand or foot, or self-will or bodily desire.

The fear of God is a topic I don't like to be reminded of. I was always taught, it meant "fear of offending God," rather than living in mortal fear and dread that at some unexpected moment, a punishing God might lash out and pay me just retribution for my sins.

What does it mean for me to *keep the reverence of God before my eyes*? How do I do this in a way that works for me, not scaring me half to death, but helpfully reminding me how to live right? I know that a proper fear of the Lord is the first step of humility, and I want to take that first step in the right direction.

From my past addictive behaviors, I know too well I need to *keep myself at every moment from sins and vices, whether of the mind, the tongue, the hands, the feet, or the self-will, and check also the desires of the flesh.* Those warnings are all right on target. For me, *the desires of the flesh* are going to be the gateway to every kind of sin and vice. That may start with careless custody of the eyes, then go on to entertaining fantasies, perhaps even thinking bad words, and then move quickly into careless stewardship of my body.

With all this in plain view, Lord, I need you to help me take that first step toward humility. Help me cultivate a healthy fear of offending you. Help me remember who I am supposed to be and who you intended me to become. Amen.

January 27, May 28, September 27

CHAPTER 7: Humility (continued)

Let us recall that we are always seen by God in the heavens, that our actions everywhere are in God's sight and are reported by angels at every hour. The prophet indicates this to us, showing that our thoughts are always present to God, saying: "God searches hearts and minds" (Ps. 7:10); and again: "The Holy One knows our thoughts" (Ps. 94:11); likewise, "From afar you know my thoughts" (Ps. 139:3); and "My thoughts shall give you praise" (Ps. 76:11). That we may take care to avoid sinful thoughts, we must always say to ourselves: "I shall be blameless in God's sight if I guard myself from my own wickedness" (Ps. 18:24).

This passage begins on a rather chilling note. Not only is God watching me, but there exists an immense spy network out there made up of numerous angels ready to report anything I do that God might have missed. If that doesn't strike the fear of God into me, what would?

But I don't think it happens quite that way, although in Benedict's time, surely the prevailing worldview saw God as a people-watcher, constantly on the lookout for bad behavior to document in some celestial logbook.

My understanding is that God is observant, yet not a spy, and that God is primarily located within every human being, including me. I have a built-in divine guidance system, called a *conscience*, which under normal circumstances functions reliably. The monitoring takes place within my own conscience, inside of me, not somewhere else. And God did not put a conscience inside of me to punish me. If I just listen, it will keep me on track.

Does God keep score? I don't think so, because God is much more focused on my efforts rather than on my successes. Thank you, Lord, for being who you are, the lover of my soul. Amen.

January 28, May 29, September 28

CHAPTER 7: Humility (continued)

Truly, we are forbidden to do our own will, for Scripture tells us: "Turn away from your desires" (Ecclus. 18:30). And in prayer too we ask that God's "will be done in us" (Matt. 6:10). We are rightly taught not to do our own will, since we dread what Scripture says: "There are ways which some call right that in the end plunge into the depths of hell" (Prov. 16:25). Moreover, we fear what is said of those who ignore this: "They are corrupt and have become depraved in their desires" (Ps. 14:1). As for the desires of the body, we must believe that God is always with us, for "All my desires are known to you" (Ps. 38:10), as the prophet tells God.

Misdirected desire and self-will are two major areas I must deal with daily in searching for a spiritual life that works. The third step, *I surrender my life and my will to my Higher Power*, is indispensable for my recovery, if I am serious about working the program.

It is significant that quite early in this chapter on humility, Benedict chooses to talk about the will. When Benedict quoted the text, "Turn away from your own will" (Ecclus. 18:30), he could never have imagined how appropriate his words would later become for addicts. The addict's will is warped. Because of already having yielded to past temptation so often, the addictive will tends to yield again and again with little—if any—reflection.

I also find it uncanny that Benedict quotes the Lord's Prayer to remind me *likewise to ask God that God's will be done in me.*

What do these insights about will and desire mean for me as I consider humility? If humility is indeed foundational to building a spiritual life, how do I learn it?

"There are ways which seem right, but the ends of them plunge into the depths of hell" (Prov. 16:25, adapted). The operative word here is *seem*. Addiction has been described as *baffling, cunning, and powerful*, and I might add, *deceptive*. What *seems* right to the addict is probably wrong, is probably an unwise choice.

Unfortunately, because of a lot of past bad choices, I dare not trust my own inclinations. But I will trust *you*, Lord, to provide me with even a few extra moments to consider whether choosing this or that activity will help or hinder me, whether something might turn out to be a stepping stone or a stumbling block to our relationship. Amen.

January 29, May 30, September 29

CHAPTER 7: Humility (continued)

We must then be on guard against any base desire, because death is stationed near the gateway of pleasure. For this reason, Scripture warns us, "Pursue not your lusts" (Sir. 18:30). Accordingly, if "the eyes of God are watching the good and the wicked" (Prov. 15:3), if at all times "the Holy One looks down from the heavens on us to see whether we understand and seek God" (Ps. 14:2); and if every day the angels assigned to us report our deeds to God day and night, then we must be vigilant every hour or, as the prophet says in the psalm, God may observe us "falling" at some time into evil and "so made worthless" (Ps. 14:3). After sparing us for a while because God is loving and waits for us to improve, we may be told later, "This you did, and I said nothing" (Ps. 50:21).

We must be on our guard, therefore, against evil desires, for death is stationed near the gateway of pleasure. Pursue not your lusts. What an opener for this section, which continues to hammer away at my misguided choices and remind me that God is watching.

I want to pretend that God isn't watching, when my lusts get the best of me, when selfish desire takes over and I again become *powerless over my dependencies and life flies out of control.* How I need at that moment to surrender my misguided will and dash to pieces those bad thoughts against you, Lord, my Rock and my salvation.

What encourages me here is Benedict's reminder that in your kindness, Lord, you wait for me: you wait for me to reform, you wait for me to improve. You are a God of many second chances. You may be watching, but you are also waiting: optimistic, hopeful, I might wager even prayerful.

What are those beautiful words from First Corinthians? "Love is patient; love is kind; love bears all things, believes all things, hopes all things; love never quits" (1 Cor. 13:4–8, adapted). You are all Love, Lord, and that's how I see my relationship with you. You are always there, yes always watching, but always rooting for me, believing that my love for you will prevail over the unruly affections of my lower nature.

Keep cheering me on, Lord, and maybe someday I'll eventually cross the finish line . . . and win. Amen.

January 30, May 31, September 30

CHAPTER 7: Humility (continued)

The second step of humility is that we love not our own will nor take pleasure in the satisfaction of our desires; rather we shall imitate by our actions that saying of Christ's: "I have come not to do my own will, but the will of the One who sent me" (John 6:38). Similarly, we read, "Consent merits punishment; constraint wins a crown."

More of the same, huh? You just won't let me off the hook with this self-will thing, now will you, Lord? You even have to remind me of your own mission on earth: "*I have come not to do my own will, but the will of the One who sent Me.*" Can I live up to such standards?

So, you're telling me that for the second degree of humility, I cannot love my own will nor take pleasure in satisfying my desires, but must instead model my life after yours? That's a pretty tall order. It gives new meaning to the title of Thomas à Kempis's book *The Imitation of Christ.* How can I imitate you that closely or follow you that faithfully?

I am sure your human nature was crying out to do things a lot differently than you actually did them, Lord. My humanity has been marked by a long history of bad habits. I am used to getting immediate gratification. But Benedict quotes another author who made the point that *self-will* (self-indulgence, giving in, yielding to temptation) brings its own particular punishment (regret, remorse, guilt, despair), whereas *constraint* (restraint, self-denial, surrender, just saying "no") merits a crown, that is, bestows the ultimate reward.

Cheap thrills don't last and offer no solutions. Help me, Lord, to make the right choices. Thank you for the grace of this hour—and please watch over me the next twenty-four. Amen.

January 31, June 1, October 1

CHAPTER 7: Humility (continued)

> The third step of humility is that we submit to the prioress or abbot in all obedience for the love of God, imitating Jesus Christ, of whom the apostle says "Christ became obedient even to death" (Phil. 2:8).

Most people don't like submitting to superiors of any sort. I must admit I'm not crazy about doing so myself. I want to call the shots. The last thing I want is to have to defer to some "authority figure" I might or might not respect, and have to do whatever I'm told.

But, literally, *for the love of God* (how often have I misused those words?), the third rung on the ladder of humility is about my *submission*. "Be subject to one another out of reverence for Christ" (Eph. 5:21).

That generally unpopular passage is talking about mutual submission within the Body of Christ. I would prefer that other people just submitted to me on a one-way basis. But unfortunately, it doesn't work that way. At different times in life I must be willing to answer to other people. In serious recovery work, it means being accountable to my sponsor. My heart must be ready to take orders rather than just give them.

Benedict reminds me that Jesus was so obedient that he even went to the cross for me. I will probably never be asked to return that favor. But I *am* asked to embrace self-denial rather than continue to pamper my addictions as I have in the past.

This third step up the ladder of humility requires an open heart: one willing to take orders, and to defer without hesitation. A humble heart will help me face the baffling nature of addiction. Keep me humble, Lord, and help me obey promptly and generously. Amen.

February 1, June 2, October 2

CHAPTER 7: Humility (continued)

> The fourth step of humility is that in this obedience under difficult, unfavorable, or even unjust conditions, our hearts quietly embrace suffering and endure it without weakening or seeking escape. For Scripture has it: "Anyone who perseveres to the end will be saved" (Matt. 10:22), and again, "Be brave of heart and rely on God" (Ps. 27:14). Another passage shows how the faithful must endure everything, even contradiction, for the sake of the Holy One, saying in the person of those who suffer, "For your sake we are put to death continually; we are regarded as sheep marked for slaughter" (Rom. 8:36; Ps. 44:22). They are so confident in their expectation of reward from God that they continue joyfully and say, "But in all this we overcome because of Christ who so greatly loved us" (Rom. 8:37). Elsewhere Scripture says: "O God, you have tested us, you have tried us as silver is tried by fire; you have led us into a snare, you have placed afflictions on our

backs" (Ps. 66:10–11). Then, to show that we ought to be under a prioress or an abbot, it adds: "You have placed others over our heads" (Ps. 66:12). In truth, those who are patient amid hardships and unjust treatment are fulfilling God's command: "When struck on one cheek, they turn the other; when deprived of their coat, they offer their cloak also; when pressed into service for one mile, they go two" (Matt. 5:39–41). With the apostle Paul, they bear with "false companions, endure persecution, and bless those who curse them" (2 Cor. 11:26; 1 Cor. 4:12).

Obeying a superior, a boss, as outlined briefly in step four, is one thing. Maybe I can get with that, in theory at least. But what about when the going gets tough? What do I do *under difficult, unfavorable, or even unjust conditions, under contradiction*? What do I do when my boss is a jerk, doesn't play fair, or when I could do a better job with one hand tied behind my back? Do I still have to obey?

In truth, when I am *patient amid hardships and unjust treatment,* I am fulfilling what you want from me as I seek to grow in humility and ultimately maintain sobriety. In recovery, I cannot afford to harbor resentments, nurse grudges, or take offense at anyone.

I must firmly resist the temptation to be resentful: obeying under duress, complying even under less than favorable conditions. To dig in my heels, assert my superiority over their legitimate authority, refusing to defer to the person in charge is a recipe for relapse.

Help me, Lord, to be humble, especially under fire. May the fire of your Holy Spirit prevail over the heat of my own unruly passions. Amen.

February 2, June 3, October 3

CHAPTER 7: Humility (continued)

The fifth step of humility is that we do not conceal from the abbot or prioress any sinful thoughts entering our hearts, or any wrongs committed in secret, but rather confess them humbly. Concerning this, Scripture exhorts us: "Make known your way to the Holy One and hope in God" (Ps. 37:5). And again, "Confess to the Holy One, for goodness and mercy endure forever" (Ps. 106:1; Ps. 118:1). So too the prophet:

"To you I have acknowledged my offense; my faults I have not concealed. I have said: Against myself I will report my faults to you, and you have forgiven the wickedness of my heart" (Ps. 32:5).

I need ongoing fifth and tenth step work in order to recover. I cannot imagine life without at least one weekly meeting where I can *admit to my Higher Power, to myself, and to someone else exactly what I've been doing wrong.* The *Rule* speaks of confession as made to one's religious superior. If I am to observe the *Rule* living out in the world, I *must* have a confessor of some kind—someone to listen and pronounce God's understanding forgiveness.

In twelve-step meetings, the group experience of confession and absolution can even be more powerful than private confession. In meetings, total and rigorous honesty is *de rigueur*. Honesty is essential for emotional healing.

I firmly believe that without confession I can make little progress toward humility. I cannot be honest *unless* I confess, and I cannot confess unless I have somewhere to do so, promptly and completely.

On more than one occasion at a meeting, I must admit I have been tempted to lie about a recent relapse. But dishonesty defeats the whole purpose of going to meetings and robs me of their benefits. I cannot reap the full benefits without my humility reaching for that fifth rung, where *I conceal none of the evil thoughts that enter my heart nor the sins I have committed in secret.*

"Confession is good for the soul." True enough. But for the recovering addict it is more than just *good*: it's *essential*. It's a rung on the ladder of humility I can ill afford to miss, lest I fall, and fall hard. Please, dear Lord, help plant both feet firmly on that rung and don't let me slip. Amen.

February 3, June 4, October 4

CHAPTER 7: Humility (continued)

The sixth step of humility is that we are content with the lowest and most menial treatment, and regard ourselves as a poor and worthless worker in whatever task we are given, saying with the prophet: "I am insignificant and ignorant, no better than a beast before you, yet I am with you always" (Ps. 73: 22–23).

Being content. Being satisfied. What a concept. Who among us is ever satisfied? When is enough ever enough? When do I finally say, I am truly satisfied and couldn't use just a little more? *Being content with the poorest and worst of everything* does not sound very appealing to me.

Goethe posed a similar question in *Faust*, when he made his pact with the devil. He said in so many words, *If I ever say I am satisfied and I have arrived, then you can haul me off to hell.* Would I be willing to sign such a similar pact?

If I am serious about working on humility, I must at some point say "That's enough." Paul said he knew how to make it whether in hardship or in luxury, in plenty or in want. Could I say the same? Isn't my pathway up that humility ladder cluttered by excessive wants rather than essential needs?

To make progress in recovery, I need to be humble enough to make it with a lot less, including certain relapse triggers that could undo my sobriety. I need to get this garbage completely out of my way. I need to do with a lot less, period. "Less is more," especially in recovery: less creature comforts that delude me into thinking I am the captain of my own ship and the master of my own destiny.

Can I, in the spirit of the *Rule* and the sixth degree of humility, *be content with the poorest and worst of everything? Can I, no matter what job is assigned me, do it and not complain*?

Humility must come first as I pursue recovery. Lord, please let me just say thanks that I have a job, and then just do whatever I am assigned. Let me *give thanks in all things*, let me embrace the humility to accept even dirty jobs with delight rather than disgust. Help me keep my feet firmly planted on this sixth rung of the ladder, Lord, as I climb toward you at the top. Amen.

February 4, June 5, October 5

CHAPTER 7: Humility (continued)

The seventh step of humility is that we not only admit with our tongues but are also convinced in our hearts that we are inferior to all and of less value, humbling ourselves and saying with the prophet: "I am truly a worm, not even human, scorned and despised by all" (Ps. 22:7). "I was exalted, then I was humbled and overwhelmed with confusion" (Ps. 88:16). And again, "It is a blessing that you have humbled me so that I can learn your commandments" (Ps. 119:71, 73).

How do I rate myself, Lord? What grade do I really assign myself? I remember in school how we would sometimes go up to the teacher after getting a test or homework back and try to negotiate a higher grade. Doing so was like saying, "I am really a lot better than you actually gave me credit for. Why not give me the higher grade I so richly deserve?"

The seventh step addresses both sides of the humility coin: what I profess publicly as well as how I really rate myself privately. I am called to honesty: to admit my character defects to others as well as to myself. I might mouth my faults with apparent humility, but hoping secretly that others will contradict me. This seventh rung of the ladder calls for something else, namely an honest match between what I say and what I think. I need both to say and to think *humility* in the same breath.

In calling me once more to complete honesty, the *Rule* here reminds me that God is God and I am just little old me. I may be made in your image and likeness, but *you only are the Lord.*

Please make me humble, Lord. Don't let me buy into the fantasy that I am large and in charge. That's when I'm really heading for trouble. Remind me that my first step toward recovery must be to *admit I am powerless over my dependencies and that my life has gone out of control.* And you can take it from there. Amen.

February 5, June 6, October 6

CHAPTER 7: Humility (continued)

The eighth step of humility is that we do only what is endorsed by the common rule of the monastery and the example set by the prioress or abbot.

This short one-sentence section presents *multum in parvo.* It offers much food for thought with very few words. Benedict makes two points: first, neither *add* nor *subtract*; second, follow the *good* examples set by leaders.

While the original intent of this section was that monastics take care neither to add to nor subtract from the seventy-three-chapter *Rule*, I also see, as a "monastic in the world," some apparent applications for myself.

What is my basic *Rule of Life*? It begins with the twelve steps. I am not free to pick and choose among them or substantially alter them. I have inherited these principles from many wiser people who came before me, and *they work if I work them*. Here the *Rule* suggests that, in the pursuit of humility, one not improvise. I am likewise cautioned not to forget my humility in working the steps, one day at a time.

Another useful point: follow the *good* example set by those at it longer than you. I never fail to be inspired by those who have been working their recovery for years. They *have fought the good fight* long and hard and are still fighting, just like me, one day at a time. They have a wealth of experience to share with me, and it would be foolish not to listen carefully.

Thank you, Lord, for this one sentence reminding me that humility requires me to adopt, not adapt twelve-step principles, as I listen and learn from the more experienced. Amen.

February 6, June 7, October 7

CHAPTER 7: Humility (continued)

> The ninth step of humility is that we control our tongues and remain silent, not speaking unless asked a question, for Scripture warns, "In a flood of words you will not avoid sinning" (Prov. 10:19), and "a talkative person goes about aimlessly on earth" (Ps. 140:12).

Silence has a hallowed and prominent place in the daily program of monasteries, much as it does in the conduct of twelve-step meetings. Even when there is a legitimate opportunity to converse, say, during a meal, monks generally don't make small talk. In the cloister one gets used to restrained speech, necessary rather than discretionary talk.

The *Rule* warns that endless chatter will not keep me from sinning. In fact, it may be more apt to get me off track. The sense here is that I can't whistle my way out of the dark, nor can I ward off temptation by filibuster. Silence *is* golden. Through it I can be in touch with the divine rather than with the trivial.

Something else here reinforces our step meeting etiquette. Benedict says, *a monastic should restrain the tongue and keep silence, not speaking until questioned.* At meetings we are to refrain from "cross talk" or from interrupting a speaker. This practice has taught me the discipline of patient listening I had never before mastered anywhere else. Restrained speech is as important to the monastery as it is to recovery.

Lord, this section says that *a talkative person goes about aimlessly on earth.* Please help me to speak less and listen more. Make me attentive to your voice as it comes forth on the lips and from the hearts of your recovering children. Amen.

February 7, June 8, October 8

CHAPTER 7: Humility (continued)

> The tenth step of humility is that we are not given to ready laughter, for it is written, "Only fools raise their voices in laughter" (Eccles. 21:23).

Taken at face value, I am afraid, Benedict's discouragement of laughter makes him out to be a sourpuss or a killjoy. My experience with Benedictines and Benedictine life has been anything but sour or joyless.

This degree of humility cautions me against boisterous laughter. I can still laugh, but I don't have to let loose with a horselaugh. The Benedictine strives for *moderation in all things*, and that includes moderate use of the voice. There is no place for stridency or coarseness in community.

Laughter, especially riotous, inappropriate laughter, can actually be just one more kind of "whistling in the dark," as suggested above. Cackling can be a cover, a blanket thrown over some issue I might not want to deal with. Instead of confronting an issue honestly, prayerfully, and reflectively, I laugh out loud about it, raucously. Or I make a stupid joke about it. Do such diversionary tactics not torpedo humility?

That the monastic not be given to ready laughter. That laughter not be my first response to something I don't want to deal with honestly is what this tenth rung of humility is all about.

Lord, please help me reflect rather than react, to listen more than to laugh. Amen.

February 8, June 9, October 9

CHAPTER 7: Humility (continued)

> The eleventh step of humility is that we speak gently and without laughter, seriously and with becoming modesty, briefly and reasonably, but without raising our voices, as it is written: "The wise are known by few words."

These thoughts continue to set forth the basic principles of the preceding section: when I speak, I need to do so gently and without unnecessary laughter; humbly and seriously; reflectively and thoughtfully. I need to use but a few, sensibly chosen words, and never hold forth bombastically.

To be a person of few words is for me to embrace a virtue. No matter how polished my rhetorical skills, I can't *talk* my way out of anything. I might, however, be able to *listen* my way out. To do that, I need to be quiet long enough to hear that *still, small voice, that whispering wind, that "sound of sheer silence"* (1 Kings 19:12).

Lord, please make me into a quieter, kinder, gentler, less loquacious person; let me seek humility and simplicity rather than the prideful purchase of every bell and whistle imaginable. Amen.

February 9, June 10, October 10

CHAPTER 7: Humility (concluded)

> The twelfth step of humility is that we always manifest humility in our bearing no less than in our hearts, so that it is evident at worship, in the oratory, the monastery or the garden, on a journey or in the field, or anywhere else. Whether sitting, walking, or standing, our heads must be bowed and our eyes cast down. Judging ourselves always guilty on account of our sins, we should consider that we are already at the fearful judgment, and constantly say in our hearts what the tax collector in the

gospel said with downcast eyes: "I am a sinner, not worthy to look up to the heavens" (Luke 18:13). And with the prophet: "I am bowed down and humble in every way" (Ps. 38:7–9; Ps. 119:107).

Now, therefore, after ascending all these steps of humility, we will quickly arrive at the "perfect love" of God which "casts out fear" (1 John 4:18). Through this love, all that we once performed with dread, we will now begin to observe without effort, as though naturally, from habit, no longer out of fear of hell, but out of love for Christ, good habit, and delight in virtue. All this God will by the Holy Spirit graciously manifest in us now cleansed of vices and sins.

To have reached this last stage of humility, Benedict considers it important for me not only to have humility in my *heart*, but also to demonstrate it by my very *appearance*.

One might argue that this could tempt me to show off how humble I am, in essence to be proud of being humble. But I see it differently. My exterior demeanor should match my interior disposition. The tax collector's posture, a humble downcast gaze as reported in the gospels, may or may not describe how I should wear my humility. Style aside, I should strive for simplicity and transparency.

At this final, twelfth stage of humility, Benedict envisions a different operating system for my way of life: I am called to operate out of love, not out of fear. *Having climbed all these steps of humility, therefore, I am expected to advance toward that perfect love of God that casts out fear.* Part of this perfect love is likewise demonstrated in the twelfth step of AA, the pass-it-on step. We show our love and gratitude for recovery by sharing with others what we have gained through the discipline of responsible living.

The ultimate goal of scaling the ladder of humility is that I emphasize love and eradicate fear. My pride fills me with all kinds of fears. My pride prevents the Perfect Love, my Higher Power, from entering and taking hold of my life.

Lord, help me to wear humility without being proud of it. Help me to trust you in all things. Help me to be so deeply wedded to your Perfect Love that I may transcend fear and transmit love. Lord, grant me the gift of humility and the grace to make it my way of life. Amen.

CHAPTER 8: The Divine Office at Night

During the winter season, that is, from the first of November until Easter, it seems reasonable to arise at the eighth hour of the night. By sleeping until a little past the middle of the night, the community can arise with their food fully digested. In the time remaining after Vigils, those who need to learn some of the psalter or readings should study them.

Between Easter and the first of November mentioned above, the time for Vigils should be adjusted so that a very short interval after Vigils will give the members opportunity to care for nature's needs. Then, at daybreak, Lauds should follow immediately.

This introductory chapter on community prayer stresses balancing my prayer life with the necessary rest I require. The clock constitutes one part of the equation; the psalter with its 150 psalms constitutes the other. Benedict's creative genius balanced a rich prayer life with the ordinary requirements of the human body, even down to a bathroom break.

Benedict thought of practically everything. He even provides preparation time for those less experienced in the assigned psalms. Then, when the community assembles, their participation becomes more meaningful.

As a non-monastic, I appreciate a prayer plan. For me, prayer is not something "I'll just get around to." Unless I have a time and a place and a plan, it won't happen. Like physical exercise, spiritual exercise requires discipline and commitment.

Especially in recovery, I know from step eleven that *I need to seek more conscious contact with my Higher Power, asking only for discernment and perseverance.* That conscious contact won't take place by itself. I need to make a plan and stay accountable to it.

Help me, Lord, as I begin to focus on how I can establish and maintain conscious contact with you, my Higher Power to whom I must surrender daily. Amen.

February 11, June 12, October 12

CHAPTER 9: The Number of Psalms at the Night Office

During the winter season, Vigils begin with the verse: "O God, open my lips and my mouth shall proclaim your praise" (Ps. 51:17). After this has been said three times, the following order is observed: Psalm 3 with doxology; Psalm 9 with a refrain, or at least chanted; an Ambrosian hymn; then six psalms with refrain.

After the psalmody, a versicle is said and the prioress or abbot gives a blessing. When all are seated on the benches, the members in turn read three selections from the book on the lectern. After each reading a responsory is sung. The doxology is not sung after the first two responsories but only after the third reading. As soon as the cantor begins to sing the doxology, let all rise from their seats in honor and reverence for the Holy Trinity. Besides the inspired books of the Old and New Testaments, the works read at Vigils should include explanations of Scripture by reputable and orthodox writers.

When these three readings and their responsories have been finished, the remaining six psalms are sung with an "Alleluia" refrain. This ended, there follows a reading from the apostle recited by heart, a versicle and the litany, that is, "Christ, have mercy." And so, Vigils are concluded.

During my last stay in the abbey of which I am an oblate, I learned to appreciate quite literally the meaning of that triple-repeated opening verse, *Lord, open my lips, and my mouth shall declare your praise.* Believe me, getting up and dressed to appear semi-conscious at 5:45 a.m. in the monastic chapel for Vigils and Lauds, I seriously needed to ask God to open my lips, still somewhat stuck together and wanting to stay that way. They needed to be pried open by divine intervention, and, after three tries, it generally worked. How human of Benedict, how typically down to earth of him, to start his monastics off with this indispensable and honest warm-up exercise.

One of the more familiar invitatory psalms is Psalm 95, although others may be substituted, especially if the morning office is truly a daily office. Psalm 95 is a favorite invitatory of mine, one I never get bored with. Somehow its richness always surprises me with some new nugget for the day. As a soul in recovery, my favorite verses always seem to be these:

> If today you hear God's voice, do not harden your hearts, as at Meribah, as on the day at Massah in the wilderness, when your ancestors tested me, and put me to the proof, though they had seen my work. (Ps. 95:7–9 NABRE)

Benedict opens his *Rule* with the simple command to *listen*. Listen and hear. If I listen carefully and shut out the distracting noises around me, the many voices competing for my attention, and choose to listen for God's voice, then I can start hearing, then I can start getting fed and directed along paths of peace and serenity.

Once I start hearing you, Lord, let me act according to your will. Let me not repeat the errors of my past, let me not try your patience, nor ignore all you have done to prove your love. Open not only my lips, but my ears, my eyes, and my heart as well. Amen.

February 12, June 13, October 13

CHAPTER 10: The Arrangement of the Night Office in Summer

From Easter until the first of November, the winter arrangement for the number of psalms is followed. But because summer nights are shorter, the readings from the book are omitted. In place of the three readings, one from the Old Testament is substituted. This is to be recited by heart, followed by a short responsory. In everything else, the winter arrangement for Vigils is kept. Thus, winter and summer, there are never fewer than twelve psalms at Vigils, not counting Psalms 3 and 95.

It is amazing in the twenty-first century to learn that in Benedict's day, one could expect an Old Testament reading be said by heart.

While this provision adjusts the prayer plan to the season, omitting three long lessons, it also shows what a different space people were in back then.

Memorization of anything, least of all prayers, is virtually nonexistent nowadays. Anything can be looked up on the Internet, or computed on a calculator. Information appears almost instantaneously. Whether this is real progress or not is debatable.

Psalm 3 also occurs here, a short but valuable psalm for persons in recovery. This psalm stresses God's ever-present protection whenever one falls under attack, wherever and whenever the baffling, cunning, and powerful nature of addiction may strike:

> O Lord, how many are my foes! Many are rising against me; many are saying to me, "There is no help for you in God." But you, O Lord, are a shield around me, my glory, and the one who lifts up my head. I cry aloud to the Lord, and he answers me from his holy hill. (Ps. 3:1–4)

The psalm concludes by saying that "deliverance belongs to the Lord" (Ps. 3:8), another one of those concise, yet powerful quotations suitable for framing.

Lord, I claim your deliverance, your protection. Come help me right now, today, tomorrow, and forever, but above all, for the next twenty-four hours. Amen.

February 13, June 14, October 14

CHAPTER 11: The Celebration of Vigils on Sundays

On Sunday the community should arise earlier for Vigils. In these Vigils, too, there must be moderation in quantity: first, as we have already indicated, six psalms are said, followed by a versicle. Then the members, seated on the benches and arranged in their proper order, listen to four readings from the book. After each reading a responsory is sung, but the doxology is added only to the fourth. When the cantor begins it, all immediately rise in reverence.

After these readings, the same order is repeated: six more psalms with refrain as before, a versicle, then four more readings and their responsories, as above. Next, three canticles from the prophets, chosen by the prioress or abbot, are said with an "Alleluia" refrain. After a versicle and the blessing of the abbot or prioress, four New Testament readings follow with their responsories, as above. After the fourth responsory, the prioress or abbot begins the hymn "We Praise You, God." When that is finished, they read from the Gospels while all stand with respect and awe. At the conclusion of the Gospel reading, all reply "Amen," and immediately the prioress or abbot intones the hymn "To You Be Praise." After a final blessing, Lauds begin.

This arrangement for Sunday Vigils should be followed at all times, summer and winter, unless—God forbid—the members happen to arise too late. In that case, the readings or responsories will have to be shortened. Let special care be taken that this not happen, but if it does, the one at fault is to make due satisfaction to God in the oratory.

Unless it should happen—God forbid—that the members be late in rising, in which case the readings or the responsories will have to be shortened. Benedict's pragmatic approach, his understanding of our weak human nature, again comes to the fore as he gives the liturgist some leeway. It strikes this modern reader as a humorous little addendum to all the details in his prayer plan, but typical of Benedict's empathy and tolerance for my frail humanity. No slave driver, no taskmaster, no demagogue, this Benedict.

Canticles are lyrical songs (*cantare*, to sing) ever present in the offices, according to season. Two verses from a canticle celebrated during Easter Season (Hosea 6:1–6) speak eloquently to the soul in recovery:

"Come, let us return to the Lord; for it is he who has torn, but he will heal us; he has struck down, and he will bind us up. . . .

Let us know, let us press on to know the Lord; his appearing is as sure as the dawn; he will come to us like the showers, like the spring rains that water the earth." (Hosea 6:1, 3)

I surely know what it is to have been torn and struck down many times by addiction. But I likewise know what it is to receive your healing touch, Lord, to be bandaged up by you, the Divine Physician, whenever I slip and fall and hurt myself again.

Step eleven urges me to get to know you, Lord, *to make conscious contact with my Higher Power*. How deeply I believe your gentle showers will wash away the hardened layers of my guilt. Amen.

February 14, June 15, October 15

CHAPTER 12: The Celebration of the Solemnity of Lauds

Sunday Lauds begins with Psalm 66, said straight through without a refrain. Then Psalm 50 follows with an "Alleluia" refrain. Lauds continues with Psalms 117 and 62, the Canticle of the Three Young Men (Dan. 3:52–56, 57–90), Psalms 148 through 150, a reading from the Apocalypse recited by heart and followed by a responsory, an Ambrosian hymn, a versicle, the Gospel canticle, the litany, and the conclusion.

The morning office on Sundays includes the marvelous last three psalms of praise in the Psalter, namely Psalms 148–150. Especially Psalm 148 is a wonderful, upbeat way to begin the first day of any week, the Lord's Day.

The praise pronounced in these three psalms seems to touch on every possible detail of nature, every entity of God's creation: angels, sun, moon, stars, waters, sea monsters, fire, hail, snow, frost, and stormy winds. The poet's universal praise doesn't stop there either, but goes on to embrace trees, mountains and hills, animals both wild and tame, creepy crawly things and flying birds, kings and princes, the young and the old, women and men.

The call to praise issued in Psalm 148 is about as comprehensive as one could imagine. Among the various ways one can pray, prayers of praise can often be the most healing, though often less practiced.

I get so used to asking you for something I need, Lord, but forget to praise and thank you first. Help me to praise you for the gift of healing that you offer us in recovery. You promise no cure, but certainly your healing, your ongoing healing for our ongoing addictions. For this hope of healing, for the promised blessings of sobriety, as a tiny part of your vast creation, God, I praise you for your limitless love and constant care. Amen.

February 15, June 16, October 16

CHAPTER 13: The Celebration of Lauds on Ordinary Days

On ordinary weekdays, Lauds are celebrated as follows. First, Psalm 67 is said without a refrain and slightly protracted as on Sunday so that everyone can be present for Psalm 51, which has a refrain. Next, according to custom, two more psalms are said in the following order: on Monday, Psalms 5 and 36; on Tuesday, Psalms 43 and 57; on Wednesday, Psalms 64–65; on Thursday, Psalms 88 and 90; on Friday, Psalms 76 and 92; on Saturday, Psalm 143 and the Canticle from Deuteronomy, divided into two sections with the doxology after each section. On other days, however, a Canticle from the prophets is said, according to the practice of the Roman Church. Next follows Psalms 148 through 150, a reading from the apostle recited by heart, a responsory, an Ambrosian hymn, a versicle, the Gospel canticle, the litany, and conclusion.

One could spend hours reflecting on the eleven assigned psalm readings for weekday mornings. We seek God's supportive presence in our lives as we try to recover from all kinds of addiction. A verse from each psalm has been lifted up for further reflection. May each verse speak to you personally, and each time you encounter this section, may the Lord enlighten afresh. "Speak, Lord, for your servants are listening."

Monday

5:3 In the morning you hear my voice; in the morning I plead my case to you, and watch.

36:7 How precious is your steadfast love, O God! All people may take refuge in the shadow of your wings.

Tuesday

43:5 Why are you cast down, O my soul, and why are you disquieted within me? Hope in God; for I shall again praise him, my help and my God.

57:1 Be merciful to me, O God, be merciful to me, for in you my soul takes refuge . . . until the destroying storms pass by.

Wednesday

64:1 Hear my voice, O God, in my complaint; preserve my life from the dread enemy.

65:3 When deeds of iniquity overwhelm us, you forgive our transgressions.

Thursday

88:4 I am counted among those who go down to the Pit; I am like those who have no help.

90:15 Make us glad as many days as you have afflicted us, and as many years as we have seen evil.

Friday

76:11 Make vows to the Lord your God, and perform them; let all who are around him bring gifts to the one who is awesome.

92:12 The righteous flourish like the palm tree, and grow like a cedar in Lebanon.

Saturday

143:2 Do not enter into judgment with your servant, for no one living is righteous before you.

CHAPTER 13: The Celebration of Lauds on Ordinary Days (concluded)

Assuredly, the celebration of Lauds and Vespers must never pass by without the prioress or abbot reciting the entire Prayer of Jesus (the Lord's Prayer) at the end for all to hear, because thorns of contention are likely to spring up. Thus warned by the pledge they make to one another in the very words of this prayer: "Forgive us as we forgive" (Matt. 6:12), they may cleanse themselves of this kind of vice. At other celebrations, only the final part of this prayer is said aloud, that all may reply: "But deliver us from evil" (Matt. 6:13).

Usually the Lord's Prayer is said not only just during morning and evening prayer but also at table prayers and of course during the Eucharist.

It is important that all hear it, *because the thorns of scandal are apt to spring up*, when there exists any disparity between forgiving others and asking forgiveness for oneself. *Forgive us our sins, as we forgive those who sin against us.* The text bears repeating.

The Lord's Prayer denotes a covenantal agreement, a two-way understanding whereby *we* agree to forgive others in direct proportion to how much we ask God to forgive *us*. That can be a tall order.

Those of us in recovery do not have to look very far to find how necessary two-way forgiveness is in our lives. In step five *I admit to my Higher Power, to myself, and to someone else exactly what I've been doing wrong.* This admission will ultimately lead me to step eight, where *I personally make amends to everyone I have harmed, unless doing so would cause them or others further harm.*

The Our Father—or the Lord's Prayer or the Prayer of Jesus—can never be said too often, no matter how it is called. It always concludes our home group meeting. For addicts in recovery and for those who love them, this prayer expresses the ultimate covenant of honesty. May we ever thus forgive. Amen.

CHAPTER 14: The Celebration of Vigils on the Anniversaries of Saints

On the feasts of saints, and indeed on all solemn festivals, the Sunday order of celebrations is followed, although the psalms, refrains, and readings proper to the day itself are said. The procedure, however, remains the same as indicated above.

A German proverb says, "One has to celebrate the feasts as they occur." All kinds of saints' feasts, major and minor, are found on the liturgical calendars followed in monasteries and elsewhere.

Such feasts are special to the monastic rhythms of life, yet both the number and order of psalms are kept constant for the sake of regularity, to observe a *regula* or Rule of Life. Consistency is key to maintaining any healthy lifestyle, whether spiritual or physical.

This feature of the *Rule* makes me think about how well I manage my own spiritual life or my recovery. Another German saying is that "In God's service, there are no holidays." That doesn't mean there are no special festivals, but it does mean I can ill afford to take a vacation from God even on holidays. If I do, my recovery runs the risk of getting onto the wrong track or, worse, getting totally derailed. The spiritual homework of recovery is a daily process, a day-to-day process, a 24-hours-at-a-time process. One cannot jump ahead. One has to live in the present.

Lord, help me to be consistently faithful and faithfully consistent in my relationship with you. Let me not yield to the temptation of taking a vacation from your presence. You certainly have yet to go off and leave me. Were you to do so, I would simply no longer exist. It's that simple. Amen.

CHAPTER 15: The Times for Saying "Alleluia"

From the holy feast of Easter until Pentecost, "Alleluia" is always said with both the psalms and the responsories. Every night from Pentecost until the beginning of Lent, it is said only with the last six psalms of Vigils. Vigils, Lauds, Prime, Terce, Sext, and None are said with "Alleluia" every Sunday except in Lent; at Vespers, however, a refrain is used. "Alleluia" is never said with responsories except from Easter to Pentecost.

The word *Alleluia* is a liturgical word. It is a joyous affirmation of God's goodness, a word of unreserved praise for the King of Kings and Lord of Lords. It occurs very frequently, even repeatedly in the monastic offices, except for the penitential season of Lent when it is omitted.

The so-called little hours of Prime, Terce, Sext, and None, which historically stood for the first, third, sixth, and ninth hours respectively, counting from six o'clock in the morning, are mentioned here in connection with the use of *Alleluia*. The little hours are like spiritual connective tissue between the two great hinges of the office known as morning (Matins) and evening prayer (Vespers). Describing the little hours in connection with the use of *Alleluia* underscores how important Benedict considered this praise word even during the lesser moments of the day.

Anytime during the day, I can make my simple *Alleluias*. Short, spontaneous, impromptu exclamations of praise are appropriate whenever I think about God or grace or healing or any other blessing in my life.

Whenever I thank you, Lord, for the last twenty-four hours of sobriety and beg you for the next twenty-four, let me begin and end each petition with the simple yet profound praise word *Alleluia*. Amen.

February 19, June 20, October 20

CHAPTER 16: The Celebration of the Divine Office during the Day

The prophet says: "Seven times a day have I praised you" (Ps. 119:164). We will fulfill this sacred number of seven if we satisfy our obligations of service at Lauds, Prime, Terce, Sext, None, Vespers, and Compline, for it was of these hours during the day that it was said: "Seven times a day have I praised you" (Ps. 119:164). Concerning Vigils, the same prophet says: "At midnight I arose to give you praise" (Ps. 119:62). Therefore, we should "praise our Creator for just judgments" at these times: Lauds,

Prime, Terce, Sext, None, Vespers, and Compline; and "Let us arise at night to give praise" (Ps. 119:164, 62).

"Seven times during the day," says the prophet, *"I have rendered you praise."* Benedict places this quotation right after his discussion on the singing or saying of the *Alleluia.* He is once again stressing a concept we came to much later, *the sanctification of time*, spreading prayer out evenly over twenty-four hours.

Prayer is not meant to be a one-shot-deal, something done all up front in the day or when day is done. Prayer cannot be distilled into a single long-acting pill taken once a day, once a week, or once a month. Rather prayer, by its very nature, is meant to be absorbed in small doses taken regularly throughout the day and night, as if to keep the potency of grace functioning in one's system. Sporadic prayer is better than no prayer at all, but generally less effective.

Seven was both a biblical and a mystical number representing perfection, completion, or fullness. While today we might classify something as a "ten," the biblical-mystical equivalent was a "seven."

Benedict, spiritual teacher par excellence, then proceeds to count it out for us, showing how the morning office (consisting of Vigils and Lauds), Prime, Terce, Sext, None, Vespers, and Compline add up to that perfect number seven.

How do I pray? Do I ever pray alone? Do I sprinkle prayer, whether structured or unstructured, throughout my day? Or do I only pray corporately on Sunday mornings in church or when attending some civic function? The *Rule* advises me to arrange my day around prayer. Help me Lord to see the wisdom of sanctifying the minutes and blessing the hours you grant me to live, to love, and to heal. Amen.

February 20, June 21, October 21

CHAPTER 17: The Number of Psalms to Be Sung at These Hours

We have already established the order for psalmody at Vigils and Lauds. Now let us arrange the remaining hours.

Three psalms are to be said at Prime, each followed by the doxology. The hymn for this hour is sung after the opening versicle, "O God, come to my assistance" (Ps. 70:2), before the psalmody begins. One reading follows the three psalms, and the hour is concluded with a versicle, "Lord, have mercy," and the dismissal.

Prayer is celebrated in the same way at Terce, Sext, and None: that is, the opening verse, the hymn appropriate to each hour, three psalms, a reading with a versicle, "Lord, have mercy," and the dismissal. If the community is rather large, refrains are used with the psalms; if it is smaller, the psalms are said without refrain.

At Vespers the number of psalms should be limited to four, with refrain. After these psalms there follow: a reading and responsory, an Ambrosian hymn, a versicle, the Gospel Canticle, the litany, and, immediately before the dismissal, the Lord's Prayer.

Compline is limited to three psalms without refrain. After the psalmody comes the hymn for this hour, followed by a reading, a versicle, "Lord, have mercy," a blessing, and the dismissal.

Two important points are made here. The first and more important one is about how the office is to begin, what opening words are to be said. Those words are not just an empty formula, but have taken on great meaning for me as I begin each daily office: *O God, come to my assistance; O Lord, make haste to help me.*

These words confess my utter helplessness as I begin to pray. They stress my need for you, Lord, to be there and make sure I am not just mouthing words, but mean what I say. These opening words come first, then the hymn, then the psalms. To charge right into the hymn would be a mistake. I must pause and invite you, Lord, to come make sense out of the words on the page.

Secondly, the *Rule* also says, don't skimp, cut short, or "piggyback" prayers: *Let three Psalms be said, separately and* not *under one "Glory be to the Father."* Benedict says, "Repeat, repeat, and repeat." Fear no redundancy. Repetition is said to be the mother of learning (*Repetitio est mater studiorum*). Repeating the doxology can never be overdone: *Glory to the Father, and to the Son, and to the Holy Spirit. As it was in the beginning, is now, and will be forever. Amen.*

Why does the Rule recommend the doxology for such frequent repetition? Because it reminds us that amidst all the "changes and chances" of this life, there is something eternal holding all things temporal together. That would be the Holy Trinity. Focusing on that mystery, repeating its formula for the eternal existence of God in three persons, somehow gets me through the unexpected valleys of life, as I "trudge the path of Happy Destiny." In recovery work, repetition is a necessary, even essential, element to internalize, sometimes even memorize, the twelve-step language. Repetition is not only the mother of *learning*, it can likewise be the mother of *nurture*, nursing us day-by-day back to wholeness. Amen.

February 21, June 22, October 22

CHAPTER 18: The Order of the Psalmody

Each of the day hours begins with the verse, "O God, come to my assistance; O Lord, make haste to help me" (Ps. 70:2), followed by the doxology and the appropriate hymn.

Then, on Sunday at Prime, four sections of Psalm 119 are said. At the other hours, that is, at Terce, Sext, and None, three sections of this psalm are said. On Monday, three psalms are said at Prime: Psalms 1, 2, and 6. At Prime each day thereafter until Sunday, three psalms are said in consecutive order as far as Psalm 20. Psalms 9 and 18 are each divided into two sections. In this way, Sunday Vigils can always begin with Psalm 21.

One could spend hours reflecting on the eighteen assigned psalms for weekday mornings. We seek God's supportive presence in our lives as we try to recover from our various addictions. I have selected one verse from each psalm for reflection. *Speak, Lord, for your servants are listening.*

Monday

1:3 They [who delight in the Lord] are like trees planted by streams of water, which yield their fruit in its season, and their leaves do not wither. In all that they do, they prosper.

2:11 Serve the Lord with fear, with trembling kiss his feet . . . happy are all who take refuge in him.

6:2 Be gracious to me, O Lord, for I am languishing; O Lord, heal me, for my bones are shaking with terror.

Tuesday

7:10 God is my shield, who saves the upright in heart.

8:5 Yet you have made [human beings] a little lower than God, and crowned them with glory and honor.

9:9 The Lord is a stronghold for the oppressed, a stronghold in times of trouble.

Wednesday

10:1 Why, O Lord, do you stand far off? Why do you hide yourself in times of trouble?

11:3 "If the foundations are destroyed, what can the righteous do?"

12:8 On every side the wicked prowl, as vileness is exalted among humankind.

Thursday

13:6 I will sing to the Lord, because he has dealt bountifully with me.

14:2 The Lord looks down from heaven on humankind to see if there are any who are wise, who seek after God.

15:1 O Lord, who may abide in your tent? Who may dwell on your holy hill?

Friday

16:5 The Lord is my chosen portion and my cup; you hold my lot.

17:8 Guard me as the apple of the eye; hide me in the shadow of your wings.

18:3 I call upon the Lord, who is worthy to be praised, so I shall be saved from my enemies.

Saturday

18:46 The Lord lives! Blessed be my rock, and exalted be the God of my salvation.

19:12 But who can detect their errors? Clear me from hidden faults.

20:7 Some take pride in chariots, and some in horses, but our pride is in the name of the Lord our God.

February 22, June 23, October 23

CHAPTER 18: The Order of the Psalmody (continued)

On Monday at Terce, Sext, and None, the remaining nine sections of Psalm 119 are said, three sections at each hour. Psalm 119 is thus completed in two days, Sunday and Monday. On Tuesday, three psalms are said at each of the hours of Terce, Sext, and None. These are the nine psalms 120–128. The same psalms are repeated at these hours daily up to Sunday. Likewise, the arrangement of hymns, readings and versicles for these days remains the same. In this way, Psalm 119 will always begin on Sunday.

These three "little" hours include the nine psalms from 120 to 128, assigned on weekdays in groupings of three. Many prayer themes present themselves in these psalms, but let us once again focus on a single verse from each, as it might speak to us as persons in recovery. May your reflections be fruitful, and may God bless you as you listen for God's message to you.

120:2 "Deliver me, O Lord, from lying lips and from a deceitful tongue."

121:7 The Lord will keep you from all evil; he will keep your life.

122:1 I was glad when they said to me, "Let us go to the house of the Lord!"

123:4 Our soul has had more than its fill of the scorn of those who are at ease, of the contempt of the proud.

124:6 Blessed be the Lord, who has not given us as prey to [our enemies'] teeth.

125:2 As the mountains surround Jerusalem, so the Lord surrounds his people, from this time on and forevermore.

126:5 May those who sow in tears reap with shouts of joy.

127:1 Unless the Lord builds the house, those who build it labor in vain.

128:1 Happy is everyone who fears the Lord, who walks in his ways.

February 23, June 24, October 24

CHAPTER 18: The Order of the Psalmody (continued)

Four psalms are sung each day at Vespers, starting with Psalm 110 and ending with Psalm 147, omitting the psalms in this series already assigned to other hours, namely, Psalms 118 through 128, Psalm 134 and Psalm 143. All the remaining psalms are said at Vespers. Since this leaves three psalms too few, the longer ones in the series should be divided: that is, Psalms 139, 144, and 145. And because Psalm 117 is short, it can be joined to Psalm 116. This is the order of psalms for Vespers; the rest is as arranged above: the reading, responsory, hymn, versicle, and canticle. The same psalms—4, 91, and 134—are said each day at Compline.

This section on Vespers and Compline is very detailed and involved, since morning prayer (Matins/Lauds) and evening prayer (Vespers) form the two major bookends of the daily office. The section bears further study, indeed. For now, let us look at the brief but highly moving service of Compline or Night Prayer. The assigned psalms are the same every day, namely Psalms 4, 91, and 134.

While Vespers may be more elaborate, with more material and detail, the shorter, simpler office of Compline packs a great deal into a short space. It is actually short enough to be memorized and said in bed before turning the light off (or blowing the candle out) as the last prayer of the day.

We know that what we go to sleep thinking about usually will "program" us for the next twenty-four hours. On that score alone, deciding to recite Compline is a wise choice. For those struggling with addictions, the night hours can often present a time of restlessness rather than restfulness.

Following once again are a few selected verses around themes that might soothe us into healthful, refreshing sleep:

4:8 I will both lie down and sleep in peace; for you alone, O Lord, make me lie down in safety.

91:5 You will not fear the terror of the night, or the arrow that flies by day.

134:1 Come, bless the Lord, all you servants of the Lord, who stand by night in the house of the Lord.

Leap Year, February 24, June 25, October 25

CHAPTER 18: The Order of the Psalmody
(concluded)

The remaining psalms not accounted for in this arrangement for the day hours are distributed evenly at Vigils over the seven nights of the week. Longer psalms are to be divided so that twelve psalms are said each night.

Above all else we urge that if people find the distribution of the psalms unsatisfactory, they should arrange whatever they judge better, provided that the full complement of one hundred and fifty psalms is by all means carefully maintained every week, and that the series begins anew each Sunday at Vigils. For members who in a week's time say less than the full psalter with the customary canticles betray extreme indolence and lack of devotion in their service. We read, after all, that our holy ancestors, energetic as they were, did all this in a single day. Let us hope that we, lukewarm as we are, can achieve it in a whole week.

How typical of Benedict once again to offer us the flexibility of adapting his *Rule*. This is all the more impressive since the psalms are so central to the offices, and since he has labored so diligently to create this grand scheme. Nonetheless he provides an out when he says, *If this distribution of the Psalms displeases anyone, arrange them otherwise, whatever way you consider better, but take care in any case that the Psalter with its full number of one hundred and fifty Psalms be chanted every week.*

Just as one is individually responsible for one's own recovery, so too is anyone free to adapt this grand prayer plan of Benedict's for daily living.

Fortunately, there have been many adaptations, including briefer versions of a daily prayer plan, abbreviations that work better for those who "live and move and have their being" outside cloister walls.

May you find your proper prayer plan. And may the Good Shepherd come right alongside, as we strive for conscious contact with our Higher Power. Amen.

February 24 (25), June 26, October 26

CHAPTER 19: The Discipline of Psalmody

We believe that the divine presence is everywhere and "that in every place the eyes of God are watching the good and the wicked" (Prov. 15:3). But beyond the least doubt we should believe this to be especially true when we celebrate the Divine Office.

We must always remember, therefore, what the prophet says: "Serve the Holy One with reverence" (Ps. 2:11), and again, "Sing praise wisely" (Ps. 47:8); and "In the presence of the angels I will sing to you" (Ps. 138:1). Let us consider, then, how we ought to behave in the presence of God and of the angels, and let us sing the psalms in such a way that our minds are in harmony with our voices.

For the Benedictine, the various hours of the daily office punctuate the day from early morning to late evening. Structured prayer is the foundation on which a coherent spiritual life is built. For the last eight chapters of his *Rule*, Benedict has painstakingly detailed exactly which psalms are to be said, when, why, and how.

The psalter, consisting of one hundred and fifty psalms, is said or sung in its entirety once a week in the monastery. Over and over again, week in, week out, these same thoughts are being recorded in the memories of monks and nuns whose mandate is *ora et labora*, pray and work.

The first word of that motto, pray, is first for a reason. Prayer must come first: before work, before play, before all else. For me as someone living outside the cloister and yet following the *Rule* as best I can, a disciplined prayer life is all the more foundational. This section emphasizes that I should pray carefully and pray well. I am reminded that I am being watched by the powers that be. Do a good job.

The direction to *sing praises wisely* and to *take part in the psalmody in such a way that our mind may be in harmony with our voice* speaks volumes about the primacy of prayer. Prayer cannot be optional or occasional. It is not the frosting on the cake, but rather the most basic ingredient of the cake itself.

Lord, if just for today, please help my *mind be in harmony with my voice*. Don't let me just mouth words or just sing lyrics. But rather *let the words of my mouth and the meditation of my heart always be acceptable in your sight, my Lord and my Redeemer*. Amen.

February 25 (26), June 27, October 27

CHAPTER 20: Reverence in Prayer

> Whenever we want to ask a favor of someone powerful, we do it humbly and respectfully, for fear of presumption. How much more important, then, to lay our petitions before the God of all with the utmost humility and sincere devotion. We must know that God regards our purity of heart and tears of compunction, not our many words (Matt. 6:7). Prayer should therefore be short and pure, unless perhaps it is prolonged under the inspiration of divine grace. In community, however, prayer should always be brief; and when the prioress or abbot gives the signal, all should rise together.

An astute observation about prayer. I am going to God and asking for an audience, asking for God's time and attention. Benedict makes the analogy to life in the world. If I am going to some bigwig and asking for their time, attention, and perhaps a favor, then I am going to be pretty careful how I approach the person. I would do so "with hat in hand," with humility and respect, not showing off or acting entitled, but with a gentle and unassuming manner.

So why should I approach God any differently? I should not be casual, careless, or sloppy when I present myself. I should not go with the attitude that God owes me, because I am such a hot shot.

But also, when I approach God, I need to be brief, not eloquent. God knows why I'm coming anyway, and God will take it from there. The prayer of a monastic is reverent but brief, never boastful or verbose. Help me too, Lord, to address you briefly, confidently, and with surrender. As the third step goes, *I surrender my life and my will to you, my Higher Power.* In that act of surrender, I come *just as I am, without one plea.* With no pretense, no diatribe, no bargaining, with just the firm belief that *whatever I ask believing, it will be granted.* Amen.

February 26 (27), June 28, October 28

CHAPTER 21: The Deans of the Monastery

> If the community is rather large, some chosen for their good repute should be made deans. They will take care of their groups of ten, managing all affairs according to the commandments of God and the orders of their prioress or abbot. Anyone selected as a dean should be the kind of person with whom the prioress or abbot can confidently share the burdens of office. They are to be chosen for virtuous living and wise teaching, not for their rank.
>
> If perhaps one of these deans is found to be puffed up with any pride, and so deserving of censure, they are to be reproved once, twice, and even a third time. Should they refuse to amend, they must be removed from office and replaced by another who is worthy. We prescribe the same course of action in regard to the subprioress or prior.

This section at face value seems specialized, addressing the administration of a larger monastery. How could it pertain to little old me out here in the world? What do *I* really have to do with *deans* or *deaneries*? The issue is the delegation of authority. When numbers grow, the need for supervision grows. A staff of eight or ten maybe I can manage. A staff of fifty or a hundred or more calls for the help of people I can count on. What no leader needs are people who will act out against policy, substituting their own agenda.

How do I fit into this part of the *Rule*? In two ways perhaps. Possibly in my job, I must in some manner delegate responsibility, but more to the point, I am someone to whom responsibilities have been delegated. *From a person to whom much has been given, much is expected in return.*

When you give me gifts, Lord, talents, blessings, abilities, and I do not manage them responsibly, then you might be moved to give them to somebody else, as in the parable of the ten talents. If I bury or abuse the gifts you have given me, I may wind up losing them.

How might I have abused your gifts, Lord, over the years? By acting out, how have I simply taken for myself what was never really mine but belonged to you? You had entrusted me with abilities I should have been using for good purposes, often for the good of others. How have I trampled all over those gifts, Lord, perverting them for my own pleasure?

These are questions for me to deal with, Lord, as I continue the inventory required in step ten, where I *examine my life and whenever I do wrong, promptly admit it.* I need to promptly admit any relapses and ongoing misuse of your gifts.

Lord, make me a better steward. Help me toward total surrender. For another twenty-four hours at least, let me claim you as the Faithful One I rely on. Amen.

February 27 (28), June 29, October 29

CHAPTER 22: The Sleeping Arrangements of Monastics

Members are to sleep in separate beds. They receive bedding as provided by the prioress or abbot, suitable to monastic life. If possible, all are to sleep in one place, but should the size of the community preclude this, they will sleep in groups of ten or twenty under the watchful care of elders. A lamp must be kept burning in the room until morning. They sleep clothed, and girded with belts or cords; but they should remove their knives, lest they accidentally cut themselves in their sleep. Thus the members will always be ready to arise without delay when the signal is given; each will hasten to arrive at the Divine Office before the others, yet with all dignity and decorum. The younger members should not have their beds next to each other, but interspersed among the elders.

On arising for worship, they will quietly encourage each other, for the sleepy like to make excuses.

To say that sleep is important would be obvious if not trite. Why does Benedict even address this topic or why should I? What does the topic of rest have to do with one's spiritual and emotional life? Like the topic of deans or priors in abbeys, we might further wonder, how does all this pertain to an addict trying to make it out in the world?

Especially those who suffer from addiction need to provide for proper rest, relaxation, down time, healthy vacations, and such. How can I get away from work for a while? Even the monastic must depart from the routine of cloister life for brief periods. Prayer is work, too, spiritual work, prescribed, as we have seen, in incredible detail in the *Rule*. Although refreshing and inspiring, prayer can still become one more agenda item, one more duty on my daily calendar.

Healing, restful sleep is a marvelous way to get away from the stranglehold of my daily agenda, to regroup, and get refreshed for the next twenty-four hours. I can ill afford to forget the HALT acronym, lest in my tiredness I forget the "T" and relapse.

To cope with the cunning nature of addiction, I need to wake up adequately refreshed for the next twenty-four hours. That may mean taking an occasional catnap. That may mean carving out some personal time off. That may mean not postponing my vacation yet again.

Getting proper rest can mean a lot of things. What does it mean for *me* to get and to stay properly rested? What lifestyle changes do I need to make?

Lord, unfortunately, so far I have done a poor job taking care of myself. Addicts don't tend to self-care that well. And worse, sometimes I don't feel I deserve a day off. But you always want me at my best, one day at a time. Give me grace to rest well, to rest in you. Amen.

February 28 (29), June 30, October 30

CHAPTER 23: Excommunication for Faults

If monastics are found to be stubborn or disobedient or proud, if they grumble or in any way despise the holy rule and defy the orders of the elders, they should be warned twice privately by them in accord with Christ's injunction (Matt. 18:15, 16). If they do not amend, they must be rebuked publicly in the presence of everyone. But if even then they do not reform, let them be excommunicated, provided that they understand the nature of this punishment. If however they lack understanding, let them undergo corporal punishment.

This passage gives me some idea how to deal with people in my life who are, in a word, a pain. In monastic community such people's faults are magnified, since you can't get away from them, at least for very long. A cloistered community by definition does practically everything together.

Out in the world where I work is where I spend most of every day. But at least after work I can escape annoying people whose behavior I find difficult to endure.

Benedict lays out reasonable measures to help change objectionable behaviors in the cloister. I most likely have no way to change the bad behavior of a coworker. Employees are not bound by monastic vows nor are they subject to much discipline. Unless I'm the boss, I have no real leverage to get people to shape up or ship out. And in today's politically correct work climate, it seems harder and harder to get rid of such troublesome people. They seem to constitute a protected species for whom no secular form of *excommunication* really exists.

What am I left to do? What alternatives do I have when people are *obstinate, or disobedient, or proud, or murmuring, or habitually violate policies and procedures, or are generally contemptuous of the orders given them*?

The truth is, the only person I can change is myself. I couldn't change other people, even if I had the authority to do so. The HALT acronym comes to mind again: I must guard against the "A" word, getting *angry* at them. I cannot afford to harbor resentments, judgment, or grudges. These surefire relapse triggers will start me feeling sorry for myself and soon I'll be acting out all over again. I cannot afford that. I do not want that.

Other people's bad behavior cannot become my problem; it has to remain theirs. They need to own it and deal with it, or not, as they choose. Fretting or whining over it will only get me in trouble.

Lord, help me pray for people who push my buttons. I surrender each one of them to you right now. Let me go about my workday focused on my own *serenity to accept the things* (including the people) *I cannot change*. Amen.

March 1, July 1, October 31

CHAPTER 24: Degrees of Excommunication

> There ought to be due proportion between the seriousness of a fault and the measure of excommunication or discipline. The prioress or abbot determines the gravity of the faults.
>
> If monastics are found guilty of less serious faults, they will not be allowed to share the common table. Members excluded from the common table will conduct themselves as follows: in the oratory they will not lead a psalm or a refrain nor will they recite a reading until they have made satisfaction, and they will take meals alone, after the others have eaten. For instance, if the community eats at noon, they will eat in midafternoon; if the community eats in midafternoon, they will eat in the evening, until by proper satisfaction pardon is gained.

Everything in life, including bad behavior, can be graded somewhere between major and minor. Here the *Rule* describes what are lesser offenses, minor infractions, or faults of a lesser degree, sometimes called *peccadilloes* or little sins.

In my own life, I need to be careful about minimizing any behavior relating to my addiction. Allowing myself a puff on a cigarette, a sip of wine, an extra helping of food, or a casual glance at a questionable magazine: any of these actions could be harmless or downright disastrous, depending on my addiction(s).

As an addict, I need to remember I am unable to control and enjoy my "drug of choice" even a little bit. It won't stop there, but will eventually lead to relapse. Before I realize what's up, once again I'm hooked.

Tolerating "lesser faults" may be lesser for others, but not for me. For me, they will soon become greater faults and turn dangerous. I cannot allow myself to be casual or careless. I can cut myself no slack, if I really want to stay clean and sober.

Lord, make me more keenly aware of even minor flirtations with my "drug of choice," flirtations that might easily lead to disaster. The earlier I get those warning signs, the more likely I might be to escape. As my ever-present Higher Power, please alert me to the triggers of relapse. Lord, let nothing undo the recovery I seek. Amen.

March 2, July 2, November 1

CHAPTER 25: Serious Faults

> Those guilty of a serious fault are to be excluded from both the table and the oratory. No one in the community should associate or converse with them at all. They will work alone at the tasks assigned to them, living continually in sorrow and penance, pondering that fearful judgment of the apostle: "Such a person is handed over for the destruction of the flesh that the spirit may be saved on the day of Jesus Christ" (1 Cor. 5:5). Let them take their food alone in the amount and at a time that the prioress or abbot considers appropriate. They should not be blessed by anyone passing by, nor should the food that is given them be blessed.

Originally, the monastic penalty for weightier faults was shunning. The operative words were exclusion, aloneness, and no community blessing. Isolation was supposed to be a time-out for the errant monk to reflect on bad behavior. Hopefully, the monastic would repent and experience a turnaround, a change of heart.

But when I am guilty of weightier faults, when I yield and ultimately lose my sobriety, isolation is the worst punishment. That's when I most need the company of compassionate listeners, the ears of my fellow travelers along *the Road of Happy Destiny*. The most pernicious thing after relapse would be to be left alone to wait for the L-word—loneliness—to do its worst (HALT).

While back in the day excommunication might have been appropriate, even helpful, for an errant monastic, I know it would be disastrous for the errant addict.

Help me, Lord, when I get lonely to call someone or to go to a meeting, lest my loneliness start me down the old pathways. *The Road of Happy Destiny* is the only healing path for me. *I know I have no other option* but to let fellowship heal what isolation would only harm. Amen.

March 3, July 3, November 2

CHAPTER 26: Unauthorized Association with the Excommunicated

If anyone, acting without an order from the prioress or abbot, presumes to associate in any way with an excommunicated member, to converse with them or to send them a message, they should receive a like punishment of excommunication.

This regulation once actually applied to the ordered discipline of a monastic community. Peer-level outreach was forbidden. In a recovery community, however, healing comes when my fellow travelers intentionally care for me in my aloneness. There is always someone there to reach out to, always someone ready to check on me, to see how I'm doing, and to share how they are doing as well.

If I get into trouble, there is no "superior" from the recovery community to tell my fellow travelers not to reach out to me, to avoid me, to leave that bad apple alone. The monastic superior perhaps did not want others to sympathize with lapsed members, lest such contact reinforce or justify bad behavior, or lest the one reaching out likewise misbehave.

Within the recovery community, it works just the opposite. Outreach is a lifeline. I never need fear that I will be shut out, shunned, or excommunicated. I am encouraged to travel together, indeed to remain in ongoing contact with my peers. From sharing comes sanity. People are encouraged, not censured, for reaching out to me. No one will ever criticize me for my faults. As fellow travelers, we are all very much in the same boat, committed to a common journey, no matter how rough the sea may get.

Lord, help me to keep reaching out, and to be grateful when others reach out to me. A phone company ad used to say, "Reach out and touch someone." That could just as well be a recovery slogan. For in reaching out and touching a fellow traveler, Lord, we touch you as well and come into powerful contact with your healing presence. *I seek more conscious contact with my Higher Power, asking only for discernment and perseverance.* Amen.

March 4, July 4, November 3

CHAPTER 27: The Concern of the Abbot and Prioress for the Excommunicated

The abbot and prioress must exercise the utmost care and concern for the wayward because "it is not the healthy who need a physician, but the sick" (Matt. 9:12). Therefore they ought to use every skill of a wise physician and send in senpectae, that is, mature and wise members who, under the cloak of secrecy, may support the wavering sister or brother, urge them to be humble as a way of making satisfaction, and "console them lest they be overwhelmed by excessive sorrow" (2 Cor. 2:7). Rather, as the apostle also says: "Let love be reaffirmed" (2 Cor. 2:8), and let all pray for the one who is excommunicated.

It is the responsibility of the abbot or prioress to have great concern and to act with all speed, discernment, and diligence in order not to lose any of the sheep entrusted to them. They should realize that they have undertaken care of the sick, not tyranny over the healthy. Let them also fear the threat of the prophet in which God says: "What you saw to be fat you claimed for yourselves, and what was weak you cast aside" (Ezek. 34:3–4). They are to imitate the loving care of Christ, the Good Shepherd, who left the ninety-nine sheep in the mountains and went in search of the one sheep that had strayed. So great was Christ's compassion for its weakness that "he mercifully placed it on his sacred shoulders" and so carried it back to the flock (Luke 15:5).

The *Rule* did make provision for the monastic community to help the disenfranchised, those at the margins of their community, but the manner of outreach was different. The superior, supported by older and more experienced monastics, bore the responsibility of getting back the lost.

Twelve-step outreach is voluntary peer outreach. We have no "superiors." My sponsor may have more time or experience in recovery, but we are peers; we all live out our sobriety one day at a time. I am as prone to fall prey to the baffling, cunning, and powerful nature of my addiction as is my sponsor, but we journey together. There are no experts. Recovery is a lifelong personal commitment, much like the vow of *stability of place*, by which Benedictine monastics promise to stay put in the community they join, and not seek another.

Lord, I claim membership in the wider recovery community, and I pledge *stability of place* to my primary group meeting, where I have so deeply shared life's darkest secrets. I need to be there. I want to be there. Heighten my commitment to do so. Make me appreciate how much the wider recovery community means to me. Thanks, Lord, for the gift of twelve-step living. Amen.

March 5, July 5, November 4

CHAPTER 28: Those Who Refuse to Amend after Frequent Reproofs

If anyone has been reproved frequently for any fault, or even been excommunicated, yet does not amend, let that member receive a sharper punishment: that is, let that monastic feel the strokes of the rod. But if even then they do not reform, or perhaps become proud and would actually defend their conduct, which God forbid, the prioress or abbot should follow the procedure of a wise physician. After applying compresses, the ointment of encouragement, the medicine of divine Scripture, and finally the cauterizing iron of excommunication and strokes of the rod, if they then perceive that their earnest efforts are unavailing, let them then apply an even better remedy: they and all the members should pray for them so that God, who can do all things, may bring about the health of the sick one. Yet if even this procedure does not heal them, then finally, the prioress or abbot must use the knife and amputate. For the apostle says: "Banish the evil one from your midst" (1 Cor 5:13); and again, "If the unbeliever departs, let that one depart" (1 Cor. 7:15), "lest one diseased sheep infect the whole flock."

Punitive measures like corporal punishment are no longer carried out in any monastic houses I know of. This is one of those antiquated historical sections of the *Rule* more reflective of an era than of the overall message of the *Rule*.

It is stunning how backwards this section is. Should not the last resort really have been the first? *If superiors see that their [punitive] efforts are of no avail, let them apply a still greater remedy, their own prayers and those of all the others, that the Lord, who can do all things, may restore health to the monastic who is sick.* In twelve-step life, I am encouraged *in my morning meditations to pray for the person who is still sick.* Intercessory prayer should always be a first resort, not a last one.

In our recovery community, thank God, we never hear such language as *Expel the evil one from your midst!* Or, *If the faithless one departs, let that one depart, lest one diseased sheep contaminate the whole flock.*

In our community, thank God, we do not *contaminate* one another. No matter how rocky our road to recovery, compassion not contamination is what's going on. If there be any contagion to report, might it not just be the contagious spirit of hope?

March 6, July 6, November 5

CHAPTER 29: Readmission of Members Who Leave the Monastery

If any community members, following their own evil ways, leave the monastery but then wish to return, they must first promise to make full amends for leaving. Let them be received back, but as a test of humility they should be given the last place. If they leave again, or even a third time, they should be readmitted under the same conditions. After this, however, they must understand that they will be denied all prospect of return.

Lord, I am so grateful for my twelve-step group. That meeting is such a regular part of my life that I have made my own monastic-like promise of *stability of place* within that community.

I feel blessed when members, for whatever reason, return. Some are absent for months. Some for over a year. Others, maybe only a couple weeks or a couple of meetings. Our group always warmly welcomes anyone back. No spirit of judgment, no critique, no blaming people for their absence. There is never need for returning members to *promise reparation for having been away, nor are they received in the lowest place, as a test of their humility.* Usually, they sit just where they used to. And it would be unthinkable, were they ever to absent themselves again, that *all way of return would be denied them.* I don't think even modern monasteries work quite this way either. Benedict was trying to protect the harmony, rhythm, and stability of a community from random interruptions during very disturbed days.

The recovery community is a fluid and dynamic one. A stable core provides the heart of any group around which many others cluster. No one issues ultimatums. No one calls the shots. Group conscience rules. All are encouraged to participate regularly, but as fellow travelers, none of us owns *the* recipe to recovery. None of us is the resident expert and none, other than our Higher Power, can ever be in charge.

You, O Lord, are in charge. You are the divine physician into whose hands I place all my hope for healing. I may never be *cured*, but I can be continually *healed* by your touch. Stretch out your hand to us, Lord, one day at a time. Amen.

March 7, July 7, November 6

CHAPTER 30: The Manner of Reproving the Young

> Every age and level of understanding should receive appropriate treatment. Therefore, as often as the young, or those who cannot understand the seriousness of the penalty of excommunication, are guilty of misdeeds, they should be subjected to severe fasts or checked with sharp strokes so that they may be healed.

Adult recovery groups do not usually include children or adolescents, nor do modern monasteries accept either group anymore. It is a wise observation, though, that *every age and degree of understanding should have its proper measure of discipline.* The current term is *age-appropriate.*

In our *delinquency* or acting out, often our biological age has little to do with how we behave. Whether young or old, addicts often *cannot understand the seriousness of the penalty of excommunication.* Few can calculate the price we pay for cutting ourselves off from reality and escaping into fantasy. Perhaps here is where *we* best qualify as *children* or *adolescents*, according to the *Rule.*

Surely, *severe fasts and harsh beatings* will not cure anything for us or anyone else, as was thought years ago and appears here in the *Rule* as another anachronism.

Perhaps a kind of fast, where we abstain from those things that lead us into temptation or deliver us into evil, is more to the point here. Perhaps some moderate self-denial might be helpful as we try only with the protection of a Higher Power, to surrender and *just say no.*

Lord, as my Higher Power, I beg you to watch over me in my spiritual immaturity, lest out of my addiction I do foolish, childish things. Be there for me and please apply age-appropriate discipline to your child gone astray. Amen.

March 8, July 8, November 7

CHAPTER 31: Qualifications of the Monastery Cellarer

As cellarer of the monastery, there should be chosen from the community someone who is wise, mature in conduct, temperate, not an excessive eater, not proud, excitable, offensive, dilatory, or wasteful, but God-fearing, and like a parent to the whole community. The cellarer will take care of everything, but will do nothing without an order from the prioress or abbot. Let the cellarer keep to those orders.

The cellarer should not annoy the members. If anyone happens to make an unreasonable demand, the cellarer should not reject that person with disdain and cause distress, but reasonably and humbly deny the improper request. Let cellarers keep watch over their own souls, ever mindful of that saying of the apostle: "They who serve well secure a good standing for themselves" (1 Tim. 3:13). The cellarer must show every care and concern for the sick, young, guests, and the poor, knowing for certain that they will be held accountable for all of them on the Day of Judgment. The cellarer will regard all utensils and goods of the monastery as sacred vessels of the altar, aware that nothing is to be neglected. Cellarers should not be prone to greed, not be wasteful and extravagant with the goods of the monastery, but should do everything with moderation and according to the order of the prioress or abbot.

The cellarer in a monastic community is the provider, the one who makes sure that all have what they need in order to function. Since monks and nuns take a vow of poverty, they are unable to provide for themselves directly. They have no money to buy nor may they order anything. They must ask the cellarer for what they need which is then provided to them.

The role of *provider* is a useful one to reflect on in recovery. Benedict wants cellarers with wisdom, mature character, *sobriety*, and the fear of God. He does not want gluttons or hotheads, the haughty or the offensive, the wasteful or the unresponsive. Finding someone with so many virtues sounds like a tall order. Yet aren't most of those virtues ones we strive for anyway in recovery?

At various times, people *provide* for us: as children, as seniors, if we become ill or handicapped. Sometimes, the state must become the provider, and for once we can thank God for taxes.

God, of course *you* are my ultimate Provider, always there to attend to my needs. The *Rule* is very godly, since it recognizes that community members have individual, not group needs. While the *Rule* does not pamper people, it does treat them individually rather than wholesale. Lord, whenever I am called on to provide for someone else's needs, whether my own family's or others', help me discern persons rather than projects, and treat each one as a unique reflection of your image and likeness. Amen.

CHAPTER 31: Qualifications of the Monastery
Cellarer (concluded)

Above all, let the cellarer be humble. If goods are not available to meet a request, the cellarer will offer a kind word in reply, for it is written: "A kind word is better than the best gift" (Sir. 18:17). Cellarers should take care of all that the prioress or abbot entrusts to them, and not presume to do what they have forbidden. They will provide the members their allotted amount of food without any pride or delay, lest they be led astray. For cellarers must remember what the Scripture says that person deserves "who leads one of the little ones astray" (Matt. 18:6).

If the community is rather large, the cellarer should be given helpers, so that with assistance it becomes possible to perform the duties of the office calmly. Necessary items are to be requested and given at the proper times, so that no one may be disquieted or distressed in the house of God.

Being humble, kind, observing boundaries are all further virtues expected of the cellarer, the provider. The provider is expected to be prompt, responsive, and not to irritate people by keeping them waiting. If additional helpers are needed, then the cellarer is to ask for them, rather than breeding unrest in the community, so that *no one may be troubled or vexed in the house of God.*

Whenever I am cast in the role of provider, Lord, even if to perform minor service duties for my group meeting, help me *fulfill with a quiet mind the office committed to me.* Even as a mini-provider with limited duties, let me always seek to foster the same serenity I need to maintain my own sobriety.

The twelfth step calls on me in any case to provide for others by sharing myself: *Grateful for a spiritual awakening from walking these steps, I share my experience with others, while practicing these principles myself, one day at a time.* Help me live that step, Lord. Amen.

CHAPTER 32: The Tools and Goods of the Monastery

The goods of the monastery, that is, its tools, clothing, or anything else, should be entrusted to members whom the prioress or abbot appoints and in whose manner of life they have confidence. The abbot or prioress will, as they see fit, issue to them the various articles to be cared for and collected after use. The prioress and abbot will maintain a list of these, so that when the members succeed one another in their assigned tasks, they may be aware of what they hand out and what they receive back.

Whoever fails to keep things belonging to the monastery clean or treats them carelessly should be reproved. If they do not amend, let them be subjected to the discipline of the rule.

In a cloister, property is shared in common, not privately owned, and the care of community property such as tools, clothing, and other recyclables is quite important. To some extent, the same is true in family households, where goods and resources, especially money, are shared in common. This places a burden on the provider, whether one or two parents, to be responsible about money.

If anyone treats the community's property in a slovenly or careless way, whether in home or cloister, correction and discipline must follow. If the teenage son drives the family car too fast and wrecks it, he has done a disservice to the whole family. If the mother gambles away the grocery money, the rest of the family doesn't eat. If the father cashes his paycheck at the bar, that family may suddenly be looking for a homeless shelter.

Addiction left untreated is insidious. It will need to be fed constantly, and guess where the funds will come from? Guess which family member will be tapping the treasury? Step eight asks that *I list every person I have harmed, and [be] ready to make amends to each and every one of them.*

Part of my recovery work means tallying up what I have wasted, how much money I have thrown away in order to self-medicate, buying whatever provided me a quick fix. In no time at all, it just left me craving more, and led to my using up yet more money to feed that monster called addiction.

Lord, help me be responsible about whatever community property to which I have access. Amen.

March 11, July 11, November 10

CHAPTER 33: Monastics and Private Ownership

Above all, this evil practice [of private ownership] must be uprooted and removed from the monastery. We mean that without an order from the prioress or abbot, no members may presume to give, receive, or retain anything as their own, nothing at all—not a book, writing tablets, or stylus—in short not a single item, especially since monastics may not have the free disposal even of their own bodies and wills. For their needs, they are to look to the prioress or abbot of the monastery, and are not allowed anything which the prioress or abbot has not given or permitted. "All things should be the common possession of all, as it is written, so that no one presumes ownership of anything" (Acts 4:32).

But if any members are caught indulging in this most evil practice, they should be warned a first and a second time. If they do not amend, let them be subjected to punishment.

Let all things be common to all, as it is written, and let no one say or assume that anything is one's own. This central notion, based on guidelines for the apostolic community as set forth by the writer of Acts, forms the heart of this teaching.

While the absolute restrictions on private ownership apply only to those living under a vow of poverty, the underlying principle can be applied more globally. Shared wealth versus private ownership also has something to do with living in relationship to others in recovery.

True, each person's recovery is their own responsibility as a lifelong, personal pursuit. Yet I also feel called to share my struggle, especially any fruitful insights, with others. My recovery may be my own, but its fruit should not be hidden, squirreled away, nor privatized from my community. I have gained something that might be of *value* or *worth* for someone else. What I *possess* is not like pens or books or food or cash, but rather skills acquired for sober living, one day at a time.

Monastics are not to have anything as their own, anything whatever; they are not permitted to have even their own bodies or wills at their own disposal. What price have *our* bodies and *our* wills paid to unlearn addictive behaviors? The core of this teaching applies powerfully to those who no longer seek to isolate themselves, to keep their body and soul locked away in fantasy, shut away from all reality.

In my home group, within my mini-community, I need to unlock and share my private self. I help not only myself by shining a light within, but I can perhaps also help others to unlock the secrets that hold them hostage. Help me, Higher Power, to have the courage to share honestly and generously with my sisters and brothers in recovery. Amen.

March 12, July 12, November 11

CHAPTER 34: Distribution of Goods According to Need

It is written: "Distribution was made as each had need" (Acts 4:35). By this we do not imply that there should be favoritism—God forbid—but rather consideration for weaknesses. Whoever needs less should thank God and not be distressed, but those who need more should feel humble because of their weakness, not self-important because of the kindness shown them. In this way all the members will be at peace. First and foremost, there must be no word or sign of the evil of grumbling, no manifestation of it for any reason at all. If, however, anyone is caught grumbling, let them undergo more severe discipline.

Benedict continues to follow out what the writer of Acts sets forth as the basis for living responsibly in community. One might call the question here, "When is enough enough?" Sharing material goods among members of a covenanted community cannot be done in cookie cutter fashion, everyone being issued exactly the same portion of everything. Benedict implies that won't work. Needs vary; some need more, some less.

A frequent guest myself in monasteries around the world, I have keenly sensed how my personal needs were being carefully accounted for.

If I needed more towels, they appeared. If I got ill, some monk came to ask me what he might bring me to make me feel better. And this caring was not even between monks in their own community, but between community and guest. Remarkable, personalized caring.

Benedict's emphasis on the significance of the individual to community is, I believe, one of his strongest suits and why his *Rule* has outlasted so many others.

Having said that about individual needs, Benedict in the next breath waxes quite emphatic about complainers. If people are being cared for this well and still gripe, something's wrong. When he says, *Above all, let not the evil of murmuring appear for any reason whatsoever in the least word or sign*, he means that amidst such tender, loving care, when such negative attitudes surface, it bespeaks a much deeper spiritual problem.

How might all this apply to my recovery? My program needs to be customized to fit who I am and how I tick. There is no cookie cutter way to sobriety. We have guidelines, outlines, and resources; but community members need to be free to work their own program. As fellow travelers, we need to make every effort to see that our sisters and brothers have all they need to create that program.

If murmuring, complaining, whining, or other expressions of our malcontent surface, more than just occasionally, then something is radically wrong. Let us encourage the chronic complainer to address that.

Lord, thanks for letting me be myself in my own recovery. Thanks for providing companions to walk with me along the *Road of Happy Destiny*. And may we engage in helpful conversation with one another along that road. Amen.

March 13, July 13, November 12

CHAPTER 35: Kitchen Servers of the Week

> The members should serve one another. Consequently, no members will be excused from kitchen service unless they are sick or engaged in some important business of the monastery, for such service increases reward and fosters love. Let those who are not strong have help so that they

may serve without distress, and let everyone receive help as the size of
the community or local conditions warrant. If the community is rather
large, the cellarer should be excused from kitchen service, and, as we
have said, those should also be excused who are engaged in important
business. Let all the rest serve one another in love.

On Saturday the ones who are completing [the kitchen] work will do
the washing. They are to wash the towels community members use to wipe
their hands and feet. Both the one who is ending service and the one who
is about to begin are to wash the feet of everyone. The utensils required for
the kitchen service are to be washed and returned intact to the cellarer,
who in turn issues them to the one beginning the next week. In this way
the cellarer will know what is handed out and what is received back.

This section makes me chuckle because it reminds me of our group meeting where opportunities for service jobs abound, even little ones like
making a pot of coffee before the meeting. How similar these kinds of
service activities are to what goes on every day in a monastery.

As a frequent guest at meals in monasteries, I have even witnessed
the abbot and retired abbot personally serving at table. (That's one duty
guests are never asked to do, probably because they don't know the routine and would be more hindrance than help.)

Why members of a monastic community would take turns at KP
seems obvious: who else would do the dirty work? Certainly not the same
people all the time. But as Benedict sees it, KP serves a higher purpose
than simply getting practical chores done, *for this service brings increase of
reward and of charity*. Who is the real beneficiary of service, the server or
the one served? *It is more blessed to give than to receive*, because experience
teaches that the giver always gets the bigger gift.

The main message here is about service, not chores: *Let the brothers
and sisters serve one another in charity*. In other words, mutual submission, mutual deference, and mutual service: *Be subject to one another out
of reverence for Christ* (Eph. 5:21). In my quest for healing, the more willing I am to make myself available to others in the recovery community,
the more I personally receive healing.

Lord, help me have the generosity of spirit to say "yes" whenever I
might be invited to serve. Amen.

March 14, July 14, November 13

CHAPTER 35: Kitchen Servers of the Week

(concluded)

An hour before mealtime, the kitchen workers of the week should each receive a drink and some bread over and above the regular portion, so that at mealtime, they may serve one another without grumbling or hardship. On solemn days, however, they should wait until after the dismissal. On Sunday immediately after Lauds, those beginning as well as those completing their week of service should make a profound bow in the oratory before all and ask for their prayers. Let the server completing the week recite this verse: "Blessed are you, O God, who have helped me and comforted me" (Dan. 3:52; Ps. 86:17). After this verse has been said three times, the server receives a blessing. Then the one beginning the service follows and says: "O God, come to my assistance; O God, make haste to help me" (Ps. 70:2). And all repeat this verse three times. When they have received a blessing, the servers begin their service.

What a humane portion of the *Rule*, and one typical of Benedict's generosity of spirit and care for the individual. He wants to make sure that *the weekly servers each receive refreshment over and above the appointed allowance, in order that at mealtime they may serve their brethren without murmuring and without excessive fatigue.*

Benedict hadn't heard of low blood sugar and what it can do to one's temperament, but he understood the principle: you can't give what you haven't got. Servers cannot serve well, if they themselves are hungry, thirsty, or otherwise unsatisfied. And not only are they to get the normal portion allotted to community members, they are to receive a larger portion, because hard work burns up calories.

The short liturgy for the weekly shift change presents a beautiful way to usher in the new duty roster and highlight the significance of service. The words, *God, come to my assistance; Lord, make haste to help me* are the opening versicle and responsory to the daily monastic hours. KP, which might seem pedestrian and far from spiritual, ranks right here alongside lofty liturgy.

In the recovery literature, one reading selection is entitled "A Vision for You," routinely recited at meetings. Benedict has just applied a similar principle here in his *Rule*: "A Vision for You" includes this simple fact: *You cannot transmit what you yourself don't have. See to it that your relationship with God is in order.*

If I am working the steps, step eleven tells me I need to *seek more conscious contact with my Higher Power, asking only for discernment and perseverance.* Just as a religious brother or sister needs enough energy to serve meals in the community refectory, and is fed appropriately according to the *Rule*, so too must I be fed adequately. Maybe I too might need even a bit more than simply the usual portion, in order to serve my sisters and brothers in the recovery community.

Help me, Lord, to work on maintaining my spiritual connection with you. Help me be faithful to meditation where I ask you to heal my brother or sister still struggling to escape the stranglehold of addiction. As you prepare me to give to others, I already know I will always get way more than I could ever give. Amen.

March 15, July 15, November 14

CHAPTER 36: The Sick

Care of the sick must rank above and before all else so that they may truly be served as Christ who said: "I was sick and you visited me" (Matt. 25:36) and "What you did for one of these least of my people you did for me" (Matt. 25:40). Let the sick on their part bear in mind that they are served out of honor for God, and let them not by their excessive demands distress anyone who serves them. Still, the sick must be patiently borne with, because serving them leads to a greater reward. Consequently, the prioress or abbot should be extremely careful that they suffer no neglect.

Let a separate room be designated for the sick, and let them be served by an attendant who is God-fearing, attentive, and concerned. The sick may take baths whenever it is advisable, but the healthy, and especially the young, should receive permission less readily.

Moreover, to regain their strength, the sick who are very weak may eat meat, but when their health improves, they should all abstain from meat as usual.

The abbot and prioress must take the greatest care that cellarers and those who serve the sick do not neglect them, for the shortcomings of disciples are their responsibility.

Part of caring in community means giving special attention to the sick. It is, as Benedict points out, a very scriptural activity, something close to Christ's heart, to his human nature. A special office within a cloistered community is that of the *infirmarian*, who sees to it that ill members of the community are properly ministered to. A community that neglects its sick is one that will soon become sick and die itself.

Benedict also makes wellness a reciprocal pursuit. He stresses the necessity of sick people contributing their part toward their own healing. Despite their discomfort, the sick may not act nasty or be demanding of their caregivers.

The *Rule* once again puts the individual in the foreground. Here, an ailing individual is permitted special diet and hygiene. A richer diet including meat along with more frequent baths (before hot water was available from a tap) are recommended, as long as legitimately needed, during the patient's illness.

The topic of wellness is certainly pertinent to recovery from addictions. Left untreated, the addict is at major risk of self-destruction. The community is responsible to provide treatment. Yet the addict must do his or her part, too, participating actively in available programs. No one else can make me well, if I am unwilling to do my part. And during the process, my own discomfort may give rise to my behaving badly toward those around me, especially those who care about my health and welfare.

Lord, make me aware of those around me who are still suffering, still sick. Let me pray for my sisters and brothers in recovery daily, and when I have the chance, let me be a source of healing for them. For when I care for one of these, the least of my sisters and brothers, you told me I was caring for you. Amen.

CHAPTER 37: The Elderly and the Young

> Although human nature itself is inclined to be compassionate toward the elderly and the young, the authority of the rule should also provide for them. Since their lack of strength must always be taken into account, they should certainly not be required to follow the strictness of the rule with regard to food, but should be treated with kindly consideration and allowed to eat before the regular hours.

What a short but beautiful reflection on both ends of the spectrum of life. Benedict speaks from his own loving heart when he says that *human nature itself is drawn to special kindness toward these times of life.* Yet for some time, even to our own day, both the very young and the very old seem often to be either abused or neglected. The sanctity of human life and the uniqueness of God's creation remain major focal points for Benedict throughout his *Rule*, and should be for us as well in our own daily *Rule of Life.*

In former times, monasteries also served as shelters for youth and senior citizens. Benedict again here wants to emphasize his concern for the individual: everyone is special in the Benedictine household, and everyone deserves special consideration.

His tenderness toward the helplessness of both young children and the elderly is important enough for Benedict to devote an entire chapter to it, even if a short one. He says, *let them by no means be held to the rigor of the Rule with regard to food.* Once again, in Benedict's view, God's creatures are unique and deserve to be treated accordingly.

Let a kind consideration be shown to them, he says. I think *kind consideration* is an absolutely marvelous phrase I want to make part of my daily vocabulary. When I get down and become tempted to grumble and complain, get into a negative frame of mind, I need to remember that phrase, *kind consideration.* Then I need to start practicing that with people I encounter every day.

If anger is a relapse trigger for addiction, and resentments lead to anger, I need to "head it off at the pass." When tempted, let me think how

I can show *kind consideration* to people to whom I might otherwise show *nasty neglect*.

Lord, help me care even half as much for other people as did Benedict. To him, as to you, everyone is special and should be treated as such. Amen.

March 17, July 17, November 16

CHAPTER 38: The Reader for the Week

Reading will always accompany the meals. The reader should not be the one who just happens to pick up the book, but someone who will read for a whole week, beginning on Sunday. After Mass and Communion, let the incoming reader ask all to pray so that God may shield them from the spirit of vanity. Let the reader begin this verse in the oratory: "O God, open my lips, and my mouth shall proclaim your praise" (Ps. 51:17), and let all say it three times. When they have received a blessing, they will begin their week of reading.

Let there be complete silence. No whispering, no speaking—only the reader's voice should be heard there. The members should by turn serve one another's needs as they eat and drink, so that no one need ask for anything. If, however, anything is required, it should be requested by an audible signal of some kind rather than by speech. No one should presume to ask a question about the reading or about anything else, "lest occasions be given to the devil" (Eph. 4:27; 1 Tim. 5:14). The abbot or prioress, however, may wish to say a few words of instruction.

Because of Communion and because the fast may be too hard for them to bear, the one who is reader for the week is to receive some diluted wine before beginning to read. Afterward they will take their meal with the weekly kitchen servers and the attendants.

Monastics will read and sing, not according to rank, but according to their ability to benefit their hearers.

One of my favorite features of monastery life is table reading during meals. I like being read to. Most adults are not read to. I remember fondly when my mother or father would read to me when I was little. It was so soothing. I could use my imagination and picture the story in my head.

And at meals in the *refectory*, the monastic dining room, it is so nice just to be quiet, to skip the small talk, skip the mindless chatter, and just listen: listen to God speaking through the reader. I can use my imagination again, as I did as a child. The only other audible sounds are the clinking of dishes or tableware. I am in an environment where I can reflect and digest more than food.

Listening to the table reader during meals is like listening to others read from recovery literature at meetings. No cross talk, no side conversations, not even whispering or interruptions of any kind are tolerated here either.

Whether in the cloister or at meetings, restraint of speech is the prescribed etiquette. In the spirit of the *Rule*, deep respect is accorded the individual, so that each may hear the voice of one's Higher Power without distraction.

The outside world is full of distractions and interruptions. It is no friendly place for meaningful reflection. It is rather a challenge to find a place of quiet. *Nature abhors a vacuum*, it has been said, and the world generally considers silence a vacuum, an empty space. People feel compelled to fill this void, with anything and everything but quiet.

Out in our noisy world, people seldom listen to one another. Generally, people go exactly counter to what our meeting etiquette requires: we do not interrupt, cross talk, or talk over others.

Lord, help me quiet down and listen. Help me focus amidst the distractions and temptations of life, amidst the many voices competing for my attention, for my affection. Let me carefully pick out your voice, as it may be heard from the lips of fellow sojourners. Amen.

March 18, July 18, November 17

CHAPTER 39: The Proper Amount of Food

For the daily meals, whether at noon or in midafternoon, it is enough, we believe, to provide all the tables with two kinds of cooked food because of individual weaknesses. In this way, the person who may not be able to eat one kind of food may partake of the other. Two kinds of cooked food, therefore, should suffice for all, and if fruit or fresh vegetables are available, a third dish may also be added. A generous pound of bread is enough for a day whether for only one meal or for both dinner and supper. In the latter case the cellarer will set aside one third of this pound and give it to the community at supper.

Should it happen that the work is heavier than usual, the abbot and prioress may decide—and they will have the authority—to grant something additional, provided that it is appropriate, and that above all overindulgence is avoided, lest anyone experience indigestion. For nothing is so inconsistent with the life of any Christian as overindulgence. Our God says: "Take care that your hearts are not weighted down with overindulgence" (Luke 21:34). The young should not receive the same amount as their elders, but less, since in all matters, frugality is the rule. Let everyone, except the sick who are very weak, abstain entirely from eating the meat of four-footed animals.

Benedictine houses are known for good food, and plenty of it. How caring that the *Rule* should prescribe for every table to have two cooked dishes, so as to account for individual dietary needs. Again, the individual's needs come to the foreground. Even a third dish is envisioned, should fresh fruit or vegetables be in season. And as if that weren't enough, at the superior's discretion something else may be added as well.

What remarkable generosity in providing for community members as well as guests. What incredible latitude, making sure no one goes hungry and all eat appropriately.

The one nutritional *caveat* is about overdoing it. A lot of food on the table is no excuse for gluttony, *for there is nothing so opposed to the Christian character as overindulgence.*

And here lies yet another key to understanding the *Rule*: moderation in all things. Balance and common sense are to prevail. The balance between prayer and work, as outlined in the daily schedule, brings an equilibrium to life. This principle may be found throughout the *Rule*, but is particularly evident here, lest one be tempted to overindulge.

Many eating disorders signal an addiction: too much eating, too little eating, fad dieting, purging, binging, and the like. Food, like alcohol or sex, is not a bad thing in itself, quite the contrary. But pushing the enve-lope even of a good thing, in order to satisfy some deeper unmet need, will ultimately become destructive.

Lord, help me balance all the good, pleasurable things in life and carry none to excess. Please help me in any areas where past behaviors have reinforced addictive or destructive patterns in my life. Help me recover and restore balance in my life. Amen.

March 19, July 19, November 18

CHAPTER 40: The Proper Amount of Drink

"Everyone has personal gifts from God, one this and another that" (1 Cor. 7:7). It is, therefore with some uneasiness that we specify the amount of food and drink for others. However, with due regard for the infirmities of the sick, we believe that a half bottle of wine is sufficient for each. But those to whom God gives the strength to abstain must know that they will earn their own reward.

The abbot or prioress will determine when local conditions, work, or the summer heat indicates the need for a greater amount. They must, in any case, take great care lest excess or drunkenness creep in. We read that monastics should not drink wine at all, but since the monastics of our day cannot be convinced of this, let us at least agree to drink mod-erately, and not to the point of excess, for "wine makes even the wise go astray" (Sir. 19:2). However, where local circumstances dictate an amount much less than what is stipulated above, or even none at all, those who live there should bless God and not grumble. Above all else we admonish them from grumbling.

This is one of the more famous chapters of the *Rule* and, compared with other monastic rules, kind of a pioneer work. Benedict's humanity shines through once again. While he sees abstinence as a lofty goal (*but those to whom God gives the strength to abstain should know that they will receive a special reward*), he is not so idealistic as to legislate it. Benedict is a realist. Maybe that's why his *Rule* is so good. He never forgets our humanity.

Benedict knows that most people are not about to embrace abstinence, and so he sanely addresses the issue, prescribing a reasonable amount of wine per day. As in the prior chapter on food, the superior is always given the latitude to increase the amount as necessary.

But just as in the last chapter, the *Rule* once again cautions us against going overboard: *Let us at least agree to drink sparingly and not to satiety.* The theme of moderation is plainly restated, and we are warned lest we abuse a good thing and make it vile.

Those of us in recovery from alcohol dependency obviously know what we need to do with this section: abstain. We have no other option. But those of us recovering from other addictions can also take a lesson from this chapter. If I am addicted to sex, love and relationships, or to food, I need to note that while any of these are healthy or harmless for the non-addict, for me they may not be abused without serious risk.

Lord, I pray as I continue to suffer the temptations of my particular dependencies. Thank you for the sanity of the Benedictine *Rule*. Yet I must continue to admit my personal powerlessness, surrender to you daily, and trust you to help me. Amen.

March 20, July 20, November 19

CHAPTER 41: The Times for Meals

From Easter to Pentecost, the monastics eat at noon and take supper in the evening. Beginning with Pentecost and continuing throughout the summer, the members fast until midafternoon on Wednesday and Friday, unless they are working in the fields or the summer heat is oppressive.

On the other days they eat dinner at noon. Indeed, the abbot or prioress may decide that they should continue to eat dinner at noon every day if they have work in the fields or if the summer heat remains extreme. Similarly, they should so regulate and arrange all matters that souls may be saved and the members may go about their activities without justifiable grumbling.

From the thirteenth of September to the beginning of Lent, they always take their meal in midafternoon. Finally, from the beginning of

Lent to Easter, they eat toward evening. Let Vespers be celebrated early enough so that there is no need for a lamp while eating, and that everything can be finished by daylight. Indeed, at all times let supper or the hour of the fast day meal be so scheduled that everything can be done by daylight.

The *Rule* is sensitive to the need to adapt all activities, including meals, to the season. There are practical reasons for doing so, since there was neither electricity nor gas to provide light or heat. Things had to be accomplished using the light of day.

What about my rhythms of life? How do I function during summer versus winter? Do I make any allowances for the different rhythms of seasonal life, or do I just go about life as if everything were the same?

If I do not seriously take seasonal rhythms into account, I run the risk of being inflexible with myself. The *Rule* makes huge allowances for flexibility. If I am working my recovery along Benedictine lines, I need to pick up on the subtle differences changing seasons may bring out in me, and respond accordingly.

Summer rhythms, summer weather, summer pace can all contribute to my slowing down a bit and getting refreshed. Or I can ignore the opportunity to relax and refresh, and just run myself into the ground, operating at winter's pace.

Lord, help me be conscious of changing seasons and aware of opportunities to adjust and adapt to life in recovery. Let me do all things in moderation, and not take myself so seriously as to miss the joys of slowing down, if only for a season. Amen.

March 21, July 21, November 20

CHAPTER 42: Silence after Compline

Monastics should diligently cultivate silence at all times, but especially at night. Accordingly, this will always be the arrangement whether for fast days or for ordinary days. When there are two meals, all will sit together immediately after rising from supper. Someone should read from the Conferences or the Lives of the early church writers or at any rate something else that will benefit the hearers, but not the Heptateuch or the Books of Kings, because it will not be good for those of weak understanding to hear these writings at that hour; they should be read at other times.

On fast days there is to be a short interval between Vespers and the reading of the Conferences, as we have indicated. Then let four or five pages be read, or as many as time permits. This reading period will allow for all to come together, in case any were engaged in assigned tasks. When all have assembled, they should pray Compline; and on leaving Compline, no one will be permitted to speak further. If monastics are found to transgress this rule of silence, they must be subjected to severe punishment, except on occasions when guests require attention or the prioress or abbot wishes to give someone a command, but even this is to be done with the utmost seriousness and proper restraint.

Zealous for silence at all times. That could be a motto or a slogan. *Silence is golden*, it is said, and there comes a time of day when silence reigns. *When they come out from Compline, no one shall be allowed to say anything from that time on.* The prayer called *Compline* or night prayer is the last of the prescribed offices of the day. It is literally meant to *complete* the day, and nothing else is supposed to follow it, except silence, lights out, and sleep.

Compline is short and the texts quite focused on anticipating a peaceful night's sleep. It is a psychologically soothing prayer office that brings a feeling of calm and protection.

The various longer readings mentioned in the *Rule* are no longer used at Compline. The service is considerably briefer, ten or fifteen minutes long. But Compline focuses on the healing power of silence, intentional silence at day's end.

To engage in anything after Compline, watching television, listening to the radio, or socializing, basically undoes the healing silence Compline has begun. Any words, any sounds are potentially counterproductive.

Lord, help me bring healing closure to every day. Music from the past bore such titles as *Now the Day Is Over* and *This Is the End of a Perfect Day*, emphasizing the beauty and necessity of closure. Help me, Lord, to bring closure on much that is past in my life. May the last prayer of the day help me connect with that *peace which passeth all understanding*. Amen.

CHAPTER 43: Tardiness at the Daily Offices
            or at Table

On hearing the signal for an hour of the Divine Office, monastics will immediately set aside what they have in hand and go with utmost speed, yet with gravity and without giving occasion for frivolity. Indeed, nothing is to be preferred to the daily office.

If at Vigils monastics come after the doxology of Psalm 95, which we wish, therefore, to be said quite deliberately and slowly, they are not to stand in their regular place in choir. They must take the last place of all, or one set apart by the prioress or abbot for such offenders, that they may be seen by them and by all, until they do penance by public satisfaction at the end of the daily office. We have decided, therefore, that they ought to stand either in the last place or apart from the others so that the attention they attract will shame them into amending. Should they remain outside the oratory, there may be those who would return to bed and sleep, or, worse yet, settle down outside and engage in idle talk, thereby "giving occasion to the Evil One" (Eph. 4:27; 1 Tim. 5:14). They should come inside so that they will not lose everything and may amend in the future.

At the day hours the same rule applies to those who come after the opening verse and the doxology of the first psalm following it: they are to stand in the last place. Until they have made satisfaction, they are not to presume to join the choir of those praying the psalms, unless perhaps the prioress or abbot pardons them and grants an exception. Even in this case, the one at fault is still bound to satisfaction.

As soon as the signal is heard. If there is anything that typifies living in a monastery, it is the ringing of the bells. They are beautiful, but also quite practical. Guests are given a printed *horarium* or daily schedule, so they know what time each activity takes place. The bells simply remind the hearer of the next activity. Monastery bells punctuate time and call attention to how well-structured time is, and how much one can accomplish if one keeps the program.

It is rude to come late for anything, especially what Benedict calls the *opus Dei*, the "work of God"—the elaborate prayer plan of the daily office, for example. On a recent monastery stay I was surprised that some community members routinely showed up late for services. I had not noticed that on my previous visit. Of course, no longer does the superior single out and ostracize latecomers as the *Rule* would indicate, but I'm reasonably sure the abbot or prioress would at least have a word in private with the frequently tardy.

In recovery meetings, we are always glad to see members show up, even if they come late. "Better late than never" we understand, especially when people are wrestling with whether they want to show up or not, and then decide to come but are a little late. No one in my group objects to that; we are just glad they came, period.

Lord, please renew within me a sense of punctuality, a sense of timeliness, a sense of obligation to be present to my fellow sojourners in recovery. Make me faithful and prompt in prayer. Help me to be on time and follow through with commitments. I know you will always be there for me, and I too want to be there for others. Amen.

March 23, July 23, November 22

CHAPTER 43: Tardiness at the Daily Offices or at Table (concluded)

But, if monastics do not come to table before the verse so that all may say the verse and pray and sit down at table together, and if this failure happens through their own negligence or fault, they should be reproved up to the second time. If they still do not amend, let them not be permitted to share the common table, but take their meals alone, separated from the company of all. Their portion of wine should be taken away until there is satisfaction and amendment. Anyone not present for the verse said after meals is to be treated in the same manner.

No one is to presume to eat or drink before or after the time appointed. Moreover, if anyone is offered something by the prioress or abbot and refuses it, then, if the monastic later wants what was refused or anything else, that one should receive nothing at all until appropriate amends have been made.

The old saying *Call me anything but late for dinner* comes to mind here. Being late for prayer services is put on an almost equal footing with being late for community meals. The meal is a kind of service in itself. There are spiritual readings, the participants observe silence, and there are prescribed prayers for both lunch and dinner.

A monastic meal is not a fast-food event. It is not something casual, where one drops in and out. It is really a liturgy in itself, an agape or love feast celebrating the heavenly banquet in miniature. That is why community meals are so important in monastic culture and why Benedict stresses being on time.

Out in the world, how often do we take practically no time at all to wolf down food? How often do we eat alone or at least not with family members? The family meal has become a rarity, something shared only at Christmas or Thanksgiving.

This section makes me think about what a meal is. Who are my important table *companions*, those with whom I break bread? Whom do I care enough about to spend that kind of time with?

Lord, help me appreciate meals as time with those closest to me. May this time always be special and unhurried. Amen.

March 24, July 24, November 23

CHAPTER 44: Satisfaction by the Excommunicated

Those excommunicated for serious faults from the oratory and from the table are to prostrate themselves in silence at the oratory entrance at the end of the celebration of the Divine Office. They should lie face down at the feet of all as they leave the oratory, and let them do this until the prioress or abbot judges they have made satisfaction. Next, at the bidding of the prioress or abbot, they are to prostrate themselves at the feet of the prioress or abbot, then at the feet of all that they may pray for them. Only then, if the prioress or abbot orders, should they be admitted to the choir in the rank the prioress or abbot assigns. Even so, they should not presume to lead a psalm or a reading or anything else in the oratory without further instructions from the prioress or abbot. In addition, at all the hours, as the Divine Office is being completed, they must prostrate themselves in the place they occupy. They will continue this form of satisfaction until the prioress or abbot again bids them cease.

Those excommunicated for less serious faults from the table only are to make satisfaction in the oratory for as long as the prioress or abbot orders. They do so until they give them the blessing and say: "Enough."

Excommunication is always a drastic measure, and was particularly so in early monastic communities. Excommunication, literally putting monastics out of community, cut them off from fellowship and marked them as existing apart from the fold.

In the early days, when monastic communities were just trying to build and separate themselves from the immoral world around them, it was necessary to exclude members who were not behaving well. The superior had to make a sharp distinction, lest boundaries between cloister and world become blurred and the monastic mission be thwarted.

In twelve-step recovery communities, there exists no manner of excommunication, no way to ostracize that I know of. Should a person fail to attend meetings regularly, that person self-excommunicates temporarily, but no one else in the program would presume to put another sojourner outside the fold, whether for relapse or for spotty attendance. Rather the opposite is true. If someone were to be absent for a while, another would reach out and try to reconnect with the person, would seek to re-incorporate rather than excommunicate.

Lord, help me stay in lively communion with my recovery community. Keep me connected and grateful for the common path we walk, that *Road of Happy Destiny*. Amen.

March 25, July 25, November 24

CHAPTER 45: Mistakes in the Oratory

> Should monastics make a mistake in a psalm, responsory, refrain, or
> reading, they must make satisfaction there before all. If they do not
> use this occasion to humble themselves, they will be subjected to more
> severe punishment for failing to correct by humility the wrong com-
> mitted through negligence. Youth, however, are to be whipped for such
> a fault.

Even for someone quite well versed in how to recite the Divine Office,
I can easily say or sing the wrong words during one of the choir offices.
When I make a mistake, it usually stands out, as these oratories are typically quite live. My mistake quite literally reverberates. Occasionally, I
might come in prematurely, not allowing sufficient pause at the asterisk
between the two halves of a psalm verse.

Any number of mistakes, whether in singing or in speaking psalms
or prayers, can intrude and bring discord to the chant. Liturgy is, after
all, a human enterprise. That means as long as mortals rather than angels
are doing the chanting, it will never be perfect. But one does one's best to
blend in with the group, so that as nearly as possible the community prays
with one voice.

The emphasis of this section is not so much on mistakes made in cor-
porate prayer, as on my willingness to acknowledge them as my own, and
not someone else's. There is always the temptation to look the other way
or hide one's faults in the crowd. "I didn't sing that wrong, they did."

Honesty about my faults is so essential to recovery, isn't it? The
fifth step calls me to *admit to my Higher Power, to myself, and to someone
else exactly what I've been doing wrong.* The issue of mistakes in worship
seems so trivial in the larger picture of faults, yet it provides a mini-test
of my personal honesty: can I be faithful and truthful even about little
things? Lord, help me tell the truth, and be honest, to myself and about
myself. Amen.

March 26, July 26, November 25

CHAPTER 46: Faults Committed in Other Matters

If monastics commit a fault while at any work—while working in the kitchen, in the storeroom, in serving, in the bakery, in the garden, in any craft or anywhere else—either by breaking or losing something or failing in any other way in any other place, they must at once come before the prioress or abbot and community and of their own accord admit their fault and make satisfaction. If it is made known through another, they are to be subjected to a more severe correction.

When the cause of the sin lies hidden in the conscience, the monastic is to reveal it only to the prioress or abbot or to one of the spiritual elders, who know how to heal their own wounds as well as those of others, without exposing them and making them public.

Benedict is still hammering away at the topic of personal honesty in all things. Here the focus is on other failings the monastic might have, other mistakes made in the discharge of one's work rather than at prayer.

The monastic, who committed some fault, broke or lost something, or broke any other sort of rule, and did not immediately and voluntarily come before both superior and community to confess and make satisfaction, was in big trouble.

Once again, the principle is not the gravity of the transgression—a broken bowl, a lost key, a forgotten chore—but personal honesty. The monastic is to be scrupulous in honesty. When an error is committed, they are to own up to it and ask forgiveness.

This applies to me, too. *You have been faithful in small things; I will put you in charge of much greater things.* I need to be careful about the little things I do wrong and own up to them, rather than minimizing them or sweeping them under the carpet. Recovery is built on a series of little steps. I can ill afford to skip any, no matter how small or insignificant they may seem. Keep me faithful in little things now, Lord, so that you may assign me more serious things later. Amen.

CHAPTER 47: Announcing the Hours for the Divine Office

It is the responsibility of the abbot and prioress to announce, day and night, the hour for the Divine Office. They may do so personally or delegate the responsibility to a conscientious member, so that everything may be done at the proper time.

Only those so authorized are to lead psalms and refrains, after the prioress or abbot according to their rank. No monastics should presume to read or sing unless they are able to benefit the hearers; let this be done with humility, seriousness, and reverence, and at the bidding of the prioress or abbot.

For me, one of the most impressive aspects of visiting a monastery is to participate in daily worship services, especially the monastic offices. Benedictines are especially noted for the quality of their sung liturgies. *No one shall presume to sing or read unless s/he can fulfill that office in such a way as to edify the hearers. Let this function be performed with humility, gravity, and reverence.*

I don't believe I have ever met a monk who also did not have a marvelous singing voice. It is hard to imagine how God gives in one neat package both a monastic as well as a musical vocation. *Who prays, sings twice* goes an old proverb, and its truth is abundant when I sit in the choir with monks and sing their liturgy with them. Next to the meals, choir offices mark the high point of my time at a monastery. Monastic liturgies are well planned and well executed. Often, however, they are somewhat complex for the non-specialist, with saints' days and such giving rise to a bit of page turning. I admit, I often have had to peek at the neighboring monk's office book to find out where we are.

Quality is perhaps the common thread connecting all this to recovery. How well the sung liturgies are prepared and executed could be likened to how well we prepare and carry off our recovery meetings. Both events have in common that they follow a prescribed format or "liturgy."

Am I prepared for my meeting? Have I looked at the recovery literature during the week? Do I know where we left off in our readings? If I am responsible for the meeting (like the abbot), do I keep things on track? Are people "singing on key," are we all on the same page, engaged with one another in a joint enterprise? My group meeting can be as quality-oriented as any monastic liturgy, or it can fall short of its potential. A well-planned meeting gives me something solid to take home and energize me for the entire week. Lord, help me to take my meetings as seriously as monastics take their prayers. Amen.

March 28, July 28, November 27

CHAPTER 48: The Daily Manual Labor

Idleness is the enemy of the soul. Therefore, the community members should have specified periods for manual labor as well as for prayerful reading.

We believe that the times for both may be arranged as follows: From Easter to the first of October, they will spend their mornings after Prime till about the fourth hour at whatever work needs to be done. From the fourth hour until the time of Sext, they will devote themselves to reading. But after Sext and their meal, they may rest on their beds in complete silence; should any members wish to read privately, let them do so, but without disturbing the others. They should say None a little early, about midway through the eighth hour, and then until Vespers they are to return to whatever work is necessary. They must not become distressed if local conditions or their poverty should force them to do the harvesting themselves. When they live by the labor of their hands, as our ancestors and the apostles did, then they are really monastics. Yet, all things are to be done with moderation on account of the fainthearted.

The Benedictine theme of *ora et labora*, pray and work, is clearly emphasized in this opening passage on daily manual labor. The twin mandates of working and praying are so carefully integrated in daily Benedictine life that the monastic can accomplish a great deal in both areas.

Prayer deals with what has been called *the sanctification of time*. The *Rule* purposely arranges the day around various times of prayer, like so many regular appointments on one's daily calendar. If *idleness is the enemy of the soul*, this enemy is dealt with deftly through the prescribed rhythms of Benedictine life, accounting for every hour of the day and night. Yet once more the familiar chord of balance is struck at the end of this passage: *Let all things be done with moderation, however, for the sake of the fainthearted*. When extra work might present itself from a windfall harvest, the *Rule* cautions monastics against overexertion or slavish adherence to the *labora* side of the equation.

Living out in the world, I am frequently tempted to work just a little bit longer, to push myself just a little bit harder. I am tempted not to come home for dinner or to curtail prayer time in favor of working longer. Out in the world, with no cloister chimes to keep me on track, it is a formidable challenge to keep the *ora* and *labora* of my life in balance.

Lord, help me living out in the world to find a way to structure my life so that it mirrors what I so admire about the cloister walk. Help me be accountable for the twenty-four hours you grant me each day. Give me time to work and time to pray, and the grace to balance both. Amen.

March 29, July 29, November 28

CHAPTER 48: The Daily Manual Labor (continued)

From the first of October to the beginning of Lent, the members ought to devote themselves to reading until the end of the second hour. At this time Terce is said and they are to work at their assigned tasks until None. At the first signal for the hour of None, all put aside their work to be ready for the second signal. Then after their meal they will devote themselves to their reading of the psalms.

During the days of Lent, they should be free in the morning to read until the third hour, after which they will work at their assigned tasks until the end of the tenth hour. During this time of Lent each one is to receive a book from the library and is to read the whole of it straight through. These books are to be distributed at the beginning of Lent.

Above all, one or two elders must surely be deputed to make the rounds of the monastery while the members are reading. Their duty is to see that no one is so apathetic as to waste time or engage in idle talk to the neglect of their reading, and so not only harm themselves but also distract others. If such persons are found—God forbid—they should be reproved a first and a second time. If they do not amend, they must be subjected to the punishment of the rule as a warning to others. Further, members ought not to associate with one another at inappropriate times.

In this section, the *Rule* lays great emphasis upon personal reading by monks and nuns over and above prescribed office readings. In fact, such reading is deemed both essential and mandatory, especially during the disciplined days of Lent.

In the early days of cloisters, this discipline was considered so significant that a kind of monastic police would enforce it, *to see that there be no lazy monastics who spend their time in idleness or gossip and not apply themselves to their reading.* Whew! That seems so old fashioned, so out of touch with modern life. Yet, how faithful *am I* to reading the literature outside of meetings to reinforce my recovery? It might be nice if someone would check on my personal reading habits. They say, "It works if you work it." A significant part of working recovery comes from reading twelve-step literature between meetings.

Lord, give me the good sense to make time during the week to *read, mark, learn, and inwardly digest* from the many sources of your wisdom: the Bible, other good books, the vast resources of recovery literature. All can help me keep walking the *Road of Happy Destiny.* Please walk along that road with me, Lord, and remind me to read more. Amen.

March 30, July 30, November 29

CHAPTER 48: The Daily Manual Labor (concluded)

On Sunday all are to be engaged in reading except those who have been assigned various duties. If any are so remiss and indolent that they are unwilling or unable to study or read, they are to be given some work in order that they may not be idle.

Those who are sick or weak should be given a type of work or craft that will keep them busy without overwhelming them or driving them away. The prioress or abbot must take their infirmities into account.

Sundays are always special on the Christian calendar. In the *Rule*, the thoughts in this passage continue to highlight reading, alongside *work* in the narrower sense. With the specter of idleness looming large, consideration is given those cloister folk who might be less than avid readers: *But if any monastics should be so negligent or shiftless that they will not or cannot study or read, let such persons be given some [other] work to do so that they will not be idle.*

These words inflict heavy judgment on the intellectually lazy, but Benedict surely must have known his constituency. In those days, cloisters were not yet the great centers of learning and scholarship they would become in later centuries. I could scarcely imagine the necessity for a literary police force to be on the prowl in any modern monastery. Despite that probable anachronism, Benedict's ongoing consideration for the individual as expressed here once again is very important. The superior is encouraged to adapt this regulation for the sick or those too weak to carry out a full program: *their weakness must be taken into consideration by the superior.* And there are all kinds of weaknesses, are there not?

Yes, Sundays have always been special to me, Lord. Let me set aside some special Sabbath time for holy reading, and let me do this as part of my recovery work. Give me time to regroup, to refresh, to learn, and pause to thank you for the last twenty-four hours. Amen.

March 31, July 31, November 30

CHAPTER 49: The Observance of Lent

The life of a monastic ought to be a continuous Lent. Since few, however, have the strength for this, we urge the entire community during these days of Lent to keep its manner of life most pure and to wash away in this holy season the negligence of other times. This we can do in a fitting manner by refusing to indulge evil habits and by devoting ourselves to prayer with tears, to reading, to compunction of heart and self-denial.

During these days, therefore, we will add to the usual measure of our service something by way of private prayer and abstinence from food or drink, so that each of us will have something above the assigned measure to offer God of our own will with the joy of the Holy Spirit (1 Thess. 1:6). In other words, let each deny oneself some food, drink, sleep, needless talking, and idle jesting, and look forward to holy Easter with joy and spiritual longing.

All should, however, make known to the prioress or abbot what they intend to do, since it ought to be done with their prayer and approval. Whatever is undertaken without the permission of the prioress or abbot will be reckoned as presumption and vainglory, not deserving a reward. Therefore everything must be done with their approval.

Benedict's tone here is prudent, fatherly, and loving toward his monks. Once again, he proves himself a splendid, sensible leader. However, Benedict the realist makes a valuable point: *Although the life of a monastic ought to have about it at all times the character of a Lenten observance, yet few have the virtue for that.* He then goes on to urge that during the actual days of Lent, the monastic add something special to the regular spiritual diet, the knowledge and consent of the abbot having been obtained beforehand.

It is worth noting that Benedict was well ahead of his time. He did not advocate *subtracting* as much as *adding*. The *Rule* does not push the misguided Lenten asceticism of giving things up, but rather recommends doing something extra, something positive: *During these days, therefore, let us increase somewhat the usual burden of our service.*

This approach applies as well to those who desire recovery. Members are always needed to volunteer for service tasks at meetings: make the coffee, check the mailbox, order supplies, keep the books. To take on any of these tasks would be to *increase somewhat the usual burden of one's service*, ultimately benefiting the members attending one's regular meeting.

And the best part of all this is that I do not have to wait until next Lent to volunteer to take on something, but can do so right away. Was it not Francis of Assisi who said *it is in giving that we receive*? Help me to serve generously, Lord, and say yes even before I am asked. Amen.

April 1, August 1, December 1

CHAPTER 50: Members Working at a Distance or Traveling

> Members who work so far away that they cannot return to the oratory at the proper time—and the prioress or abbot determines that is the case—are to perform the Divine Office where they are, and kneel out of reverence for God.
>
> So too, those who have been sent on a journey are not to omit the prescribed hours but to observe them as best they can, not neglecting their measure of service.

Trips away from home are no excuse. Oh, I could claim I couldn't find a meeting, or I was too busy, or I didn't like the local group I tried a couple of times. "I'll wait till I get home to my regular group." Sound familiar? One could complain, "The group chemistry was different." Excuses? I think so. The path of least resistance: do nothing. But eventually I will have to pay the price for not keeping up my program, not working my steps. Let me paraphrase this part of the *Rule* for those of us in recovery: *Those working at a great distance who cannot get to their regular meeting at the proper time shall perform the work of recovery wherever they happen to be, bending their wills in reverence before their Higher Power.*

Lord, I acknowledge that serious recovery means a lifelong commitment. Help me not make excuses about attending meetings or about saying my prayers, about doing the work and continually asking for your grace to surrender, one day at a time. Let any of my excuses be clearly labeled as such. Amen.

April 2, August 2, December 2

CHAPTER 51: Members on a Short Journey

> If members are sent on some errand and expect to return to the monastery that same day, they must not presume to eat outside, even if they

receive a pressing invitation, unless perhaps the prioress or abbot has ordered it. Should they act otherwise, they will be excommunicated.

The emphasis here is on the centrality of the home, the base community to which I belong. I will be tempted to prolong my workday, stay out, eat out, remain away longer than necessary from those who love me. Long trips are one thing. One has to make allowances when one is far away from home. But how many times have I stayed away from my family, or even part of my family, opting to eat out, when I could have had a sandwich with them at home instead? Someone once said on his deathbed that he never regretted not having spent more time at the office; but he surely *did* regret not having spent more time with those who love him.

When am I *expected to return the same day*? That is often largely up to me. I can stay out and work as long as I think or say I have to. But is that prudent? Is that loving? Is that advisable? Wouldn't it be better just to spend a little more time with family or community, rather than simply go it alone? Addicts often isolate themselves from the people who love them most.

Lord, help me take every opportunity I can to eat with, and therefore literally be a *companion* with those closest to me. Help me not delude myself with excuses why I need to be elsewhere, when I could just as well be with them. Don't let me regret later that I didn't spend more time with friends and family. Help me say yes to all that right now. Amen.

April 3, August 3, December 3

CHAPTER 52: The Oratory of the Monastery

The oratory ought to be what it is called, and nothing else is to be done or stored there. After the Divine Office, all should leave in complete silence and with reverence for God, so that anyone who may wish to pray alone will not be disturbed by the insensitivity of another. Moreover, if at other times some choose to pray privately, they may simply go in and pray, not in a loud voice, but with tears and heartfelt devotion. Accordingly, those who do not pray in this manner are not to remain in the oratory after the Divine Office, as we have said; then they will not interfere with anyone else.

The oratory, sometimes called the monastic chapel, is the center of the religious community's spiritual life. Whether the community is large or of more modest size, the chapel is generally a cozy, intimate place, rather than a cavernous church such as might be connected to an abbey. The oratory is a private place, generally restricted to the monastic community, with room for a few guests, but not many.

The choir offices are said or sung there, and it is an accessible place if during the day community members wish to go in and pray. Benedict emphasizes that this chapel not be an "all-purpose room," one used for concerts, lectures, meetings, and the like. This is to be solely a place of prayer. With prayer and work as the two sides of the monastic coin, this prayer side is not to be downplayed or diluted in any way.

Out in the world, we need our own oratories. Prayer is so essential to recovery because I need to establish and maintain *conscious contact with my Higher Power*. Such contact will not be effective if it is a casual, catch-as-catch-can affair. Even if I am not a cloistered monastic whose day is conveniently planned around prayer, I too need to have my special prayer time and place. I need my "prayer chair," a place dedicated to prayer, like my assigned stall in the oratory. Whatever time of day or night that works for me, I need to be faithful to it and be there to pray.

Lord, I know a relationship between us won't just "happen." I have to make talking with you a regular part of my life. Please help me be faithful to prayer, and not just in crisis but as a routine part of daily life. Amen.

April 4, August 4, December 4

CHAPTER 53: The Reception of Guests

All guests who present themselves are to be welcomed as Christ, who said: "I was a stranger and you welcomed me" (Matt. 25:35). Proper honor must be shown to all, "especially to those who share our faith" (Gal. 6:10) and to pilgrims.

Once guests have been announced, the prioress or abbot and the community are to meet them with all the courtesy of love. First of all, they are to pray together and thus be united in peace, but prayer must always precede the kiss of peace because of the delusions of the devil.

All humility should be shown in addressing a guest on arrival or departure. By a bow of the head or by a complete prostration of the body, Christ is to be adored and welcomed in them. After the guests have been received, they should be invited to pray; then the abbot or prioress or an appointed member will sit with them. The divine law is read to all guests for their instruction, and after that every kindness is shown to them. The prioress or abbot may break their fast for the sake of a guest, unless it is a day of special fast which cannot be broken. The members, however, observe the usual fast. The abbot or prioress shall pour water on the hands of the guest, and the abbot or prioress with the entire community shall wash their feet. After washing they will recite this verse: "God, we have received your mercy in the midst of your temple" (Ps. 48:10).

Great care and concern are to be shown in receiving poor people and pilgrims, because in them more particularly Christ is received; our very awe of the rich guarantees them special respect.

There is perhaps no greater hallmark of a Benedictine community than hospitality, the reception of guests in a monastery. Whenever guests arrive, the red carpet is rolled out, as has been my experience. The theological basis is set forth as the first words of this section: *let all guests who arrive be received like Christ.* No matter who is present, regardless how extended or how brief their stay, they are to be treated like Christ, and that says it all.

Monastic communities are close-knit families whose activities provide important opportunities for bonding between members. But no number of in-house activities ever eclipses guests or leaves them adrift. There is always a guestmaster to shepherd guests and see to their needs. Again, the Benedictine cares for the guest as if it were Jesus knocking at the door.

In recovery meetings, I have seen the same kind of welcoming hospitality shown to newcomers as well as returnees. My group exudes special warmth. I felt it when I turned up there for the first time. Now an established member of that same recovery community, I sense the warm welcome we extend to those joining us.

As this section of the *Rule* indicates, the superior is to allow his or her regular schedule to be interrupted to welcome and orient arriving guests. In a similar way, as trusted servants we take newly arriving guests aside at their first meeting in order to familiarize them with how our recovery community works.

Lord, make me ever sensitive to newcomers and guests. Regardless how my human nature might react to a new arrival, let me welcome each as if I were welcoming you personally. Amen.

April 5, August 5, December 5

CHAPTER 53: The Reception of Guests (concluded)

The kitchen for the abbot and prioress and guests ought to be separate, so that guests—and monasteries are never without them—need not disturb the community when they present themselves at unpredictable hours. Each year, two monastics who can do the work competently are to be assigned to this kitchen. Additional help should be available when needed, so that they can provide this service without grumbling. On the other hand, when the work slackens, they are to go wherever other duties are assigned them. This consideration is not for them alone, but applies to all duties in the monastery; members are to be given help when it is needed, and whenever they are free, they work wherever they are assigned.

The guest quarters are to be entrusted to a God-fearing member. Adequate bedding should be available there. The house of God should be in the care of members who will manage it wisely.

No monastics are to speak or associate with guests unless they are bidden; however, if the members meet or see guests, they are to greet them humbly, as we have said. They ask for a blessing and continue on their way, explaining that they are not allowed to speak.

Refreshment and lodging are the basic ingredients for hospitality. The *Rule* provides a separate kitchen and guesthouse so that the lives of community members are not disrupted by the constant comings and goings of guests. This custom is frequently modified in modern monasteries. Some do have separate guest facilities; some, house guests on certain corridors of the cloister; others give guests rooms right next to community members. Again, individual monasteries are free to adapt this custom. Much is dictated by the size of buildings, many constructed for larger communities years ago. Kitchen arrangements are also not always separate today. Guests may now eat in the refectory with the monks or nuns. Everything depends on the cloister rules established by the individual monastic house.

Regardless of any particular community's customs, the bottom line is always about making the guest feel warmly welcomed, while yet preserving peace and solitude for the regular community. While a fine line to walk, it is surely one well-trodden and well-refined over centuries.

As a person in recovery, I have very much enjoyed being an overnight guest in monasteries, places where I could pray and reflect, hope and heal. I pray that more and more persons engaged in twelve-step work avail themselves of the resources of monasteries. I know that these communities will reach out in love to those who are seeking. Amen.

April 6, August 6, December 6

CHAPTER 54: Letters or Gifts

In no circumstances are monastics allowed, unless the prioress or abbot says they may, to exchange letters, blessed tokens, or small gifts of any kind, with their parents or anyone else, or with another monastic. They must not presume to accept gifts sent them even by their parents without previously telling the prioress or abbot. If the prioress or abbot orders acceptance, they still have the power to give the gift to whomever; and the one for whom it was originally sent must not be distressed, "lest occasion be given to the devil" (Eph. 4:27; 1 Tim. 5:14). Whoever presumes to act otherwise will be subjected to the discipline of the rule.

One of the privileges a person surrenders when entering a religious order is that of unrestricted personal privacy. Sending or receiving letters we take for granted as a constitutional right. People have no right to say whether I receive mail, or do they? No one can censor my mail, or can they? Historically, that right was surrendered when one entered a religious order. It falls under the vow of obedience to the superior. In modern-day monasteries, the regulations around mail will vary, based on what type of community it is. As usual, details are left to the discretion of the superior, but at least the card is on the table. Monastics under vows do not retain all the rights and privileges they had on the outside.

As to the receiving of gifts, something else comes into play, namely living under voluntary poverty. Monks and nuns are not allowed to own anything. Property is held in community, where the community owns it all and individual members own nothing.

So even if a parent or relative gives something to their son or daughter, it still must be cleared with the superior. That is a right they surrender when they enter and embrace community life. Again, in the practical order, it would be rare for a superior to say no, unless the gift were out of proportion to monastic lifestyle (a new Porsche, a yacht, the keys to a summer cottage). But whether the superior's policies on gifts are strict or lenient, the monastic is still bound to obey them. And the fact that gifts given for one person might wind up being given to another monastic doesn't change the basic fact that all property belongs to the entire community, regardless who may have use of it at any given time.

Is there perhaps anything here for someone in recovery? I might well consider whether every message I receive helps me along the road to recovery. Or I might also think more carefully about certain kinds of gifts. What is motivating the giver? What might she or he expect in return? Is this gift good for me? Unfortunately, I have no abbot or prioress to make that call, but I do have a sponsor with whom I need to be rigorously honest about anything that might potentially sabotage recovery.

While maybe not directly applicable, this whole section still gives me pause to think more critically about what comes my way and what I allow into my life. It makes me ponder how some gifts might affect me. God grant me a moment's pause to reflect before I receive or accept anything. Amen.

April 7, August 7, December 7

CHAPTER 55: Clothing and Footwear

The clothing distributed to the members should vary according to local conditions and climate, because more is needed in cold regions and less in warmer. This is left to the discretion of the prioress or abbot. We believe that for each monastic a cowl and tunic will suffice in temperate regions; in winter a woolen cowl is necessary, in summer a thinner or worn one; also a scapular for work, and footwear—both sandals and shoes.

Monastics must not complain about the color or coarseness of all these articles, but use what is available in the vicinity at a reasonable cost. However, the prioress and abbot ought to be concerned about the measurements of these garments that they not be too short but fitted to the wearers.

Whenever new clothing is received, the old should be returned at once and stored in a wardrobe for the poor. To provide for laundering and night wear, every member will need two cowls and two tunics, but anything more must be taken away as superfluous. When new articles are received, the worn ones—sandals or anything old—must be returned.

Those going on a journey should get underclothing from the wardrobe. On their return they are to wash it and give it back. Their cowls and tunics, too, ought to be somewhat better than those they ordinarily wear. Let them get these from the wardrobe before departing, and on returning put them back.

What a difference there would be to put my clothes closet side by side with one of those of the early monks. I would be embarrassed at the multiple pairs of shoes and multiple everything else I had accumulated and never weeded out. How barebones the monastic wardrobe is, and yet how sensible. How wasteful and unnecessary are my many pieces of the same articles of clothing. I shudder to think of poor people who don't even have one article of which I have five or ten. It is time for some soul-searching here, and for some serious closet "pruning" with speedy delivery to a local clothing outlet for the poor.

Lord, make my heart grateful for all your blessings in my life. Let me embrace just a fraction of that simplicity of life the *Rule* calls for, so that I may share my abundant blessings with those far less fortunate. If it is in giving that we receive, by giving to others I ask in exchange only for your healing touch. Amen.

April 8, August 8, December 8

CHAPTER 55: Clothing and Footwear (concluded)

> For bedding monastics will need a mat, a woolen blanket, and a light covering as well as a pillow.
>
> The beds are to be inspected frequently by the prioress or abbot, lest private possessions be found there. Anyone discovered with anything not given by the prioress or abbot must be subjected to very severe punishment. In order that this vice of private ownership may be completely uprooted, the prioress or abbot is to provide all things necessary: that is, cowl, tunic, sandals, shoes, belt, knife, stylus, needle, handkerchief, and writing tablets. In this way every excuse of lacking some necessity will be taken away.
>
> The abbot and prioress, however, must always bear in mind what is said in the Acts of the Apostles: "Distribution was made as each had need" (Acts 4:35). In this way the prioress and abbot will take into account the weakness of the needy, not the evil will of the envious; yet in all their judgments they must bear in mind God's retribution.

It is striking in this section that in the early days of monasticism, the superior was instructed to act as chief inspector, making sure monastics were adhering to regulations. The issue at hand was private ownership, something strictly forbidden when one promises to live in voluntary poverty.

The superior had the obligation to inspect for contraband as well as to provide for the essentials. Nothing in the *Rule*, however, was inflexible. If someone was judged to be "weaker" and therefore in need of more, the superior could adjust and be flexible, bearing in mind the apostles' policy that *distribution was made to each according as anyone had need.*

When we consider our modern world and all the "stuff" we accumulate, material goods we collect and never seem to dispose of, this section gives me genuine pause. Do I really need all the things I own? And are these things helping or hindering me from keeping closer contact with my Higher Power? Is it not *in giving that we receive*, and by extension, by giving up some possessions that I learn how to surrender?

We have no abbot or prioress playing detective to see whether we are hoarding, but I ought to do some soul searching on this myself and examine my conscience about my possessions. What is really more important to me: my material or my spiritual welfare? Lord, help me come up with an honest answer. Amen.

April 9, August 9, December 9

CHAPTER 56: The Prioress's or Abbot's Table

> The table of the prioress or abbot must always be with guests and travelers. Whenever there are no guests, it is within the superior's right to invite anyone of the community they wish. However, for the sake of maintaining discipline, one or two seniors must always be left with the others.

One of the traditional treats of being a guest in the monastic refectory is to be placed at the head table where the abbot and prior sit. It is an honor accorded the guest, who represents Christ. If Jesus were to arrive for a meal, one would not place him at some distant table, but would surely seat him nearest the host. So it is with table hospitality shown to guests.

Where do I place visitors in my life? Are they important or secondary at my table? I hope that whether it is seating someone literally at my dining room table or giving them a place in my life, I treat them as I would treat Jesus and give them a prominent rather than a secondary place. Help me be sensitive to how I place and therefore how I rate others who come into my life, if even for a brief visit. Amen.

April 10, August 10, December 10
CHAPTER 57: The Artisans of the Monastery

If there are artisans in the monastery, they are to practice their craft with all humility, but only with the permission of the prioress or the abbot. If one of them becomes puffed up by skillfulness in the craft, and feels that they are conferring something on the monastery, they are to be removed from practicing the craft and not allowed to resume it unless, after manifesting humility, they are so ordered by the prioress or abbot.

Whenever products of these artisans are sold, those responsible for the sale must not dare to practice any fraud. Let them always remember Ananias and Sapphira, who incurred bodily death (Acts 5:1–11), lest they and all who perpetrate fraud in monastery affairs suffer spiritual death.

The evil of avarice must have no part in establishing prices, which should, therefore, always be a little lower than people outside the monastery are able to set, "so that in all things God may be glorified" (1 Pet. 4:11).

Attitude is so important in spiritual life. No matter what our talents, we need to regard them with humility. God certainly has gifted men and women throughout the ages with artistic abilities over a wide spectrum of the arts. But the common truth is: they didn't endow themselves with these, God did. Gifted persons need to polish and perfect a gift, but the basic gift came from God, not from us.

Here the *Rule* questions my attitude toward my talent. Am I haughty about how well I can do something? Do I behave as if it were my own personal property? Am I *proud* of it in the wrong sense, or do I go about practicing it with genuine humility?

If I am inappropriately proud about my artistic abilities, then the vice of greed may creep in and tempt me to reap a windfall profit from it. If I am humble about it, recognizing it as God's gift and not my own invention, then I can relax about more modest compensation.

No matter what my human abilities may be, they all belong to God, and I need to behave accordingly. *Pride goes before the fall.* Lest I fall, Lord, make me humble about whatever I do that is special. Amen.

April 11, August 11, December 11

CHAPTER 58: The Procedure for Receiving Members

Do not grant newcomers to the monastic life an easy entry, but, as the apostle says, "Test the spirits to see if they are from God" (1 John 4:1). Therefore, if someone comes and keeps knocking at the door, and if at the end of four or five days has shown patience in bearing harsh treatment and difficulty of entry, and has persisted in the request, then that one should be allowed to enter and stay in the guest quarters for a few days. After that, the person should live in the novitiate, where the novices study, eat, and sleep.

A senior chosen for skill in winning souls should be appointed to look after the newcomer with careful attention. The concern must be whether the novice truly seeks God and shows eagerness for the Divine Office, for obedience, and for trials. The novices should be clearly told all the hardships and difficulties that will lead to God.

If they promise perseverance in stability, then after two months have elapsed let this rule be read straight through to them, and let them be told: "This is the law under which you are choosing to serve. If you can keep it, come in. If not, feel free to leave." If they still stand firm, they are to be taken back to the novitiate, and again thoroughly tested in all patience. After six months have passed, the rule is to be read to them, so that they may know what they are entering. If once more they stand firm, let four months go by, and then read this rule to them again. If after due reflection they promise to observe everything and to obey every command given them, let them then be received into the community. But they must be well aware that, as the law of the rule establishes, from this day they are no longer free to leave the monastery, nor to shake from their neck the yoke of the rule which, in the course of so prolonged a period of reflection, they were free either to reject or accept.

We find an interesting contrast here between the relatively easy and laidback reception of guests and the reception accorded those aspiring to embrace monastic life. The rigorous and painstaking process as outlined resembles an obstacle course. The various stages of testing are seen as nec essary to eliminate those who are not genuinely called to this demanding lifestyle. The holy persistence required gives the seeker the opportunity for deep introspection and brutal self-honesty. Am I truly called to make this commitment? Am I willing to pay the price? Am I ready for such a level of sacrifice?

Many of these same questions could just as well apply to my quest for clean and sober living. Am I a casual participant in my recovery program, or am I prepared to engage fully and work it for a radical change of life?

Lord, grant me the depth of commitment to stay the course and respond to your healing. Let me carefully observe the rules for recovery, and let me do so, one day at a time. Amen.

April 12, August 12, December 12

CHAPTER 58: The Procedure for Receiving Members (concluded)

When they are to be received, they come before the whole community in the oratory and promise stability, fidelity to the monastic life, and obedience. This is done in the presence of God and the saints to impress on the novices that if they ever act otherwise, they will surely be condemned by the one they mock.

They state their promise in a document drawn up in the name of the saints whose relics are there and of the prioress or abbot, who is present. Novices write out this document themselves, or if they are illiterate, then they ask someone else to write it for them, but they put their mark to it and with their own hand lay it on the altar. After they have put it there, the novice begins the verse: "Receive me, O God, as you have promised, and I shall live; do not disappoint me in my hope" (Ps. 119:16). The whole community repeats the verse three times, and adds the doxology. Then the novices prostrate themselves at the feet of each member to ask prayers, and from that very day they are to be counted as one of the community.

If they have any possessions, they should either give them to the poor beforehand, or make a formal donation of them to the monastery, without keeping back a single thing for themselves, well aware that from that day they will not have even their own body at their disposal. Then and there in the oratory, they are to be stripped of everything of their own that they are wearing and clothed in what belongs to the monastery. The clothing taken from them is to be put away and kept safely in the wardrobe, so that, should they ever agree to the devil's suggestion and leave the monastery—which God forbid—they can be stripped of the clothing of the monastery before they are cast out. But that document of theirs which the prioress or abbot took from the altar should not be given back to them but kept in the monastery.

The concluding section of this chapter assumes the aspirant has been successful in their persistence and is ready to make a formal commitment. Aspirants promise *stability, fidelity to monastic life, and obedience*. One's commitment is worded most seriously, must be written out in longhand, and personally placed on the altar. This entire process underscores how grave and permanent a commitment the new monastic is making. Yet Benedict in his wisdom has thought through the terms of this commitment. What if the monk or nun leaves? What happens then? The *Rule* even speaks to this eventuality, right down to clothing issues.

For those of us in recovery, monastic promises hold much wisdom. *Stability of place* translated in our terms means my permanent commitment to a particular twelve-step group, to a particular meeting time and place, to a particular group of fellow sojourners, my own community-in-recovery. *Fidelity [to recovery life]*, in our situation, means an ongoing commitment to work my program seriously, not casually. *Obedience*, adapted to our program, suggests the concept of mutual accountability, to my sponsor as well as to my group.

There are indeed some powerful parallels between joining a monastic community and joining a recovery community. Both require heavy-duty commitment. We know we can't *control and enjoy* our addiction; it will eventually overtake and control us. Nor can the religious seeker make a casual commitment to some kind of monastic life or other in general. A

Benedictine monk or nun must always publicly and formally commit to a specific community.

Lord, help me take my recovery pilgrimage just as seriously as those who make the cloister walk. And thanks to Benedict for reminding me how serious both enterprises are. Amen.

April 13, August 13, December 13

CHAPTER 59: The Offering of Children by Nobles or by the Poor

> If a member of the nobility offers a child to God in the monastery, and the child is too young, the parents draw up the document mentioned above; then, at the presentation of the gifts, they wrap the document itself and the child's hand in the altar cloth. That is how they make their offering.
>
> As to their property, they either make a sworn promise in this document that they will never personally, never through an intermediary, nor in any way at all, nor at any time, give the child anything or afford the child the opportunity to possess anything; or else, if they are unwilling to do this and still wish to win their reward for making an offering to the monastery, they make a formal donation of the property that they want to give to the monastery, keeping the revenue for themselves, should they so desire. This ought to leave no way open for the child to entertain any expectations that could deceive and lead to ruin. May God forbid this, but we have learned from experience that this can happen.
>
> Poor people do the same, but those who have nothing at all simply write the document and, in the presence of witnesses, offer their child with the gifts.

This section of the *Rule* is now historical, since the practice no longer exists of dropping children off at monasteries and consigning them to this life. What might this portion of the *Rule* have to offer for those in recovery?

Certainly, these youngsters very early received a wonderful, holy, and nurturing environment in which to live. They got much more here than they could have on the outside, as far as living close to God. The monastery of those early days was surely rigorous and no walk in the park, yet it would have provided excellent training at an early stage of child development. Whether they stayed on and entered the communities or whether they left and reentered the world, what these children learned here surely prepared them well for life.

When I think back over the lifelong course of my addiction, when I get to know younger people in the program, I wish I had gotten into twelve-step work much earlier. I wish I had been aware that what had been plaguing me all those years was an *addiction*, not just a way of life. Had someone "dropped me off" at a meeting, like these young children had been dropped off at monasteries, signed over to their care, maybe things would have gone better. At least I would have been exposed to using the tools for sober living. But life cannot be lived in the subjunctive mood, in the hypothetical: *If it had been different, I would (not) have . . .* and so on. Life must be lived in the here and now, in the indicative mood, that which *indicates* reality. *God, grant me the serenity to accept the things I cannot change . . .*

I was called rather late in life to recovery. Well, better late than never. Please help this old dog, O God, to learn new tricks, strategies which can become ways to sober living. I thank you for having called me to sobriety, no matter how late, perhaps at my eleventh hour. However long, however short that journey may be, I trust you will walk beside me along the *Road of Happy Destiny*. Amen.

April 14, August 14, December 14

CHAPTER 60: The Admission of Priests to the Monastery

If any ordained priest asks to be received into a male monastery, do not agree too quickly. However, if he is fully persistent in his request, he must recognize that he will have to observe the full discipline of the rule without any mitigation, knowing that it is written: "Friend, what have you come for?" (Matt. 26:50). He should, however, be allowed to stand next to the abbot, to give blessings, and to celebrate the Eucharist, provided that the abbot bids him. Otherwise he must recognize that he is subject to the discipline of the rule, and not make any exceptions for himself, but rather give everyone an example of his humility. Whenever there is a question of an appointment or of any other business in the monastery, he takes the place that corresponds to the date of his entrance into the community, and not that granted him out of respect for his priesthood.

Any clerics who similarly wish to join the community should be ranked somewhere in the middle, but only if they, too, promise to keep the rule and observe stability.

But if he is quite persistent in his request, let him know that he will have to observe the whole discipline of the rule and that nothing will be relaxed in his favor. One of the common misconceptions about religious orders, especially monastic communities like the Benedictines, is that the order is made up primarily of priests. The Order of St. Benedict is not primarily a priest's order, such as the Jesuits, the Society of Jesus, for example. Benedict wrote this to warn secular or diocesan priests who aspired to becoming Benedictines not to expect the red carpet to be rolled out for them. Just because they had already been ordained priests did not make them some kind of superior religious. These men, like all other aspirants, would enter primarily as monks, not as clergy.

A young man enters a male monastery and after passing various stages of discernment eventually becomes a solemnly professed monk. After he has made that permanent commitment and sworn perpetual vows, the abbot may then sponsor him for ordination, if he has already completed seminary; or if the monk has not, the abbot may send him on for further studies. To enter a Benedictine monastery is to become a monk first, and possibly, but not necessarily, a priest later, at the discretion of the abbot and the need of the community.

While at face value this section might seem totally unrelated to recovery work, there is at least one parallel. Benedict wrote this section from his experience that some priests of his time considered themselves privileged characters, a cut above ordinary applicants to monasteries. Clericalism, the attitude that the ordained are the experts (something not entirely dead today either), runs completely counter to the culture of monastic humility. Here is the connection to the recovery community: here there are no experts either. So-and-so might have been in recovery for twenty years. So-and-so might have had ten or more years' sobriety. Yet so-and-so might just as easily fall from grace in the next twenty-four hours. Each of us can only go it one day at a time. No matter how long we've been at it, none of us is an expert.

The clericalism Benedict was putting down is good for me to hear. No matter the length of my sobriety, I am an equal with my brother or sister sitting next to me who might have twenty-four hours or less.

Lord, give me an extra dose of humility, lest I get prideful about whatever sobriety I might have today. My sister or brother may have just fallen. *There, but for your grace, go I.* Help me do at least the third thing the prophet Micah asked, "to do justice, and to love kindness, and *to walk humbly with [my] God*" (Micah 6:8). Amen.

April 15, August 15, December 15

CHAPTER 61: The Reception of Visiting Monastics

Visiting monastics from far away will perhaps present themselves and wish to stay as guests in the monastery. Provided they are content with the life as they find it, and do not make excessive demands that upset the monastery, but are simply content with what they find, they should be received for as long a time as they wish. They may indeed with all humility and love make some reasonable criticisms or observations, which the prioress or abbot should prudently consider; it is possible that God guided them to the monastery for this very purpose.

The Benedictine vow of stability of place (*stabilitas loci*) again comes into focus. It is possible on sufficient grounds for monastics to transfer their vow of *stabilitas* to another monastery. Such a transfer might have to do with the shifting charism or call on a particular monastic's life.

For example, a visiting monastic who has spent considerable time as a guest in another monastery, might see the hand of God in all this and come to realize that their original call has shifted with time. The ministry of the abbey visited might be more in line with the new call. Clearly, given one's vow of stability, one is not allowed to shift randomly from place to place, as the gyrovagues whom Benedict condemns (RB 1:10 ff.). But there can be valid reasons for shifting one's membership from one monastery to another.

The visiting monastic, however, is cautioned early in this section. When newly arrived, the visiting monk or nun is apt to notice things right away that differ from their own monastery. The *Rule* bids this visitor at the outset to *be content with the customs of the place as they are and not disturb the monastery by superfluous demands.* These are wise words. They basically take us back to Benedict's aversion to griping, complaining, or murmuring about whatever we don't like. Benedict teaches that being a monastic and being a constant complainer are incompatible.

If the visiting monastic can make some constructive criticism, the *Rule* says, fine. If not, refrain from negative remarks. What this passage says to me as a person in recovery is that I, too, should withhold rash judgment. I am far too quick to render my expert opinion on just about anything and everyone. I tend to rush to judgment, only later getting to know the person better, really liking them, and then feeling rather stupid.

Lord, help me withhold judgment for a good long time, maybe forever? Help me listen more, as the first word of the *Rule* advises. Keep me open and humble as I meet new people and encounter new things. Grant me more patience and time to reflect. Amen.

April 16, August 16, December 16

CHAPTER 61: The Reception of Visiting Monastics (concluded)

If, however, they have shown that they are not the kind of persons who deserve to be dismissed, let them, on their request, be received as a member of the community. They should even be urged to stay, so that others may learn from their example, because wherever we may be, we are in the service of the same God. Further, the prioress or abbot may set such a person in a somewhat higher place in the community, if they see that they deserve it. The prioress or abbot has the power to set any one of them above the place that corresponds to their date of entry, if they see that their life warrants it.

The prioress or abbot must, however, take care never to receive into the community anyone from another known monastery, unless the prioress or abbot of that community consents and sends a letter or recommendation, since it is written: "Never do to another what you do not want done to yourself" (Tob. 4:16).

This concluding section on visiting monks who might feel called to join the new community they are visiting, presents a double-edged sword. It recalls a short pamphlet on etiquette entitled *Guest or Pest?* This section begins with the visitor who is a pest: the perpetual complainer or the rotten apple. *But if as a guest the monastic was found exacting or prone to vice, not only should they be denied membership in the community, but they should even be politely requested to leave, lest others be corrupted.* Sound familiar?

The significantly longer final part of this section is devoted to the brighter prospect of a new monastic who will be both a positive and productive asset rather than an accident-waiting-to-happen. No community needs a loose cannon ready to fire without warning. Benedict emphasizes the positive while at the same time being cautiously realistic about people's foibles.

What about you and me? I think, as persons in recovery, we need to be very careful whom we let into our lives, into our community of confidants. To be in recovery is to be vulnerable. Until we really get to know people, especially new people we encounter in twelve-step meetings, we should perhaps follow the biblical maxim of being *wise as serpents and gentle as doves.* We need not rush to judgment about a fellow sojourner (or anyone else we might meet outside either), yet we ought not be so foolish as to make someone a fast friend who might eventually undermine our sobriety. Another maxim warns:

A little learning is a dangerous thing.
Drink deeply or taste not the Pierian spring.

While remaining open to new people, I must likewise reflect on how they might enhance or imperil my recovery.

Lord, grant me a discerning as well as a compassionate spirit. Amen.

CHAPTER 62: The Priests of the Monastery

Any abbot of a male monastery who asks to have a priest or deacon ordained should choose from his monks one worthy to exercise the priesthood. The monk so ordained must be on guard against conceit or pride, must not presume to do anything except what the abbot commands him, and must recognize that now he will have to subject himself all the more to the discipline of the rule. Just because he is a priest, he may not therefore forget the obedience and discipline of the rule, but must make more and more progress toward God.

He will always take the place that corresponds to the date of his entry into the monastery, except in his duties at the altar, or unless the whole community chooses and the abbot wishes to give him a higher place for the goodness of his life. Yet, he must know how to keep the rule established for deans and priors; should he presume to act otherwise, he must be regarded as a rebel, not as a priest. If after many warnings he does not improve, let the bishop be brought in as a witness. Should he not amend even then, and his faults become notorious, he is to be dismissed from the monastery, but only if he is so arrogant that he will not submit to or obey the rule.

Should he presume to act otherwise, let him be judged not as a priest but as a rebel. Once again, the theme of equality in monastery life is reemphasized. Ordained monks take their places in the choir stalls right next to lay religious. Their priesthood is no license to act out or act up. In Benedictine community life no one is special because all are special.

It may be helpful to remember that Benedict was a *lay* abbot and never ordained a priest. Perhaps his wariness to admit priests grew from his contact with clergy who considered themselves a cut above simple monks.

Benedict wanted to prevent any such pride or sense of superiority from contaminating community, even by spelling out penalties for offensive priests who might suffer delusions of grandeur. A priest may *preside* at the liturgy, but the whole community celebrates together, whether

Eucharist or the Divine Office. All *con*celebrate as equal members of one community. We are "one together, together one" when we submerge our egos in favor of sharing life together.

Some in recovery from multiple addictions, or with higher education or relatively long-term sobriety, consider themselves "experts" in twelve-step living. They sometimes feel they are a cut above people who suffer from only one addiction. That recalls the arrogant priest among humble monks who is eventually disciplined for his rebellious nature.

Lord, you are the only true expert, my Higher Power. Keep me humble. Help me resist ever coming across as a twelve-step expert. Let me just take my place alongside my companions in the choir stalls of recovery. Amen.

April 18, August 18, December 18

CHAPTER 63: Community Rank

Monastics keep their rank in the monastery according to the date of their entry, the virtue of their lives, and the decision of the abbot or prioress. The prioress or abbot is not to disturb the flock entrusted to them nor make any unjust arrangements, as though they had the power to do whatever they wished. They must constantly reflect that they will have to give God an account of all their decisions and actions. Therefore, when the members come for the kiss of peace and for Communion, when they lead psalms or stand in choir, they do so in the order already existing among them or decided by the abbot or prioress. Absolutely nowhere shall age automatically determine rank. Remember that Samuel and Daniel were still boys when they judged their elders (1 Sam. 3; Dan. 13:44–62). Therefore, apart from those mentioned above whom the abbot or prioress have for some overriding consideration promoted, or for a specific reason demoted, all the rest should keep the order of their entry. For example, someone who came to the monastery at the second hour of the day must recognize that they are junior to someone who came at the first hour, regardless of age or distinction. The young, however, are to be disciplined in everything by everyone.

One of the ironic aspects about Benedictine life for me today as a non-monastic is the traditional emphasis on one's rank or order in community. Having just considered equality in community, that priests for example do not trump simple monks, we now are confronted with a practice that at face value seems contradictory.

Except for those already mentioned, therefore, whom the abbot or prioress have promoted by a special decision or demoted for definite reasons, all the rest shall take their order according to the time of their entrance.

Movement and placement by order of seniority does seem anachronistic, if not in outright conflict with the principle of equality in community. But all that aside, how might this monastic tradition have something positive to say to those in recovery?

The answer has to do with basic human respect. I need to respect those who have worked at recovery longer than I. These are my seniors, as it were, yet no experts. I ought to honor those who rank before me, simply because they have worked longer at recovery.

Seniors in long-term recovery are not unlike monastics who have made a similar lifelong commitment. The addict's or codependent's recovery community is the ploughshare taken up but never abandoned. No matter how hard the struggle, with help from my Higher Power I can persist and persevere.

Lord, help me honor those who have been in long-term recovery. Grant me longevity in that battle which *knows no rest, until we rest in you.* For my *seniors*, Lord, give me a grateful and loving heart. Amen.

April 19, August 19, December 19

CHAPTER 63: Community Rank (concluded)

The younger monastics, then, must respect their elders, and the elders must love their juniors. When they address one another, no one should be allowed to do so simply by name: rather, the elders call the younger "sister" or "brother" and the younger members call their elders "nonna" or "nonnus," which are translated as "venerable one." But the abbot and prioress, because we believe that they hold the place of Christ, are to be called "abbot" or "prioress" not for any claim of their own, but out of honor and love for Christ. They for their part, must reflect on this and in their behavior show themselves worthy of such honor.

Wherever members meet, the junior asks the elder for a blessing. When older members come by, the younger ones rise and offer them a seat, and do not presume to sit down unless the older one bids them. In this way, they do what the words of Scripture say: "They should each try to be the first to show respect for the other" (Rom. 12:10).

In the oratory and at table, the young are kept in rank and under discipline. Outside or anywhere else, they should be supervised and controlled until they are old enough to be responsible.

Wherever members meet, the junior asks the elder for a blessing. What a wonderful custom. Before the assigned reader for the day reads in the dining room, that monastic bows toward the abbot or prioress or whoever is presiding at the head table, and says or sings, "Your blessing, please."

In my contacts with senior brothers and sisters in recovery, those not necessarily older, but like monastics, people who have entered the recovery community well before I did, I like to ask for their prayers. I can remember calling my sponsor once on the phone from a shopping mall quite some distance from home, asking for his counsel in a moment of temptation. I likewise sought his blessing by asking him to pray for me. He did so right then and there over the phone.

We certainly can and ought to reach out to our peers in recovery. Moreover, we need to be in touch with our "seniors" in community, begging their blessing, counsel, and support.

Help me do this on a more regular basis, Lord. Move me to enlist their prayers and their wisdom. Amen.

April 20, August 20, December 20

CHAPTER 64: The Election of a Prioress or Abbot

In choosing an abbot or prioress, the guiding principle should always be that the one placed in office be the one selected either by the whole community acting unanimously out of reverence for God, or by some part of the community no matter how small, which possesses sounder judgment. Goodness of life and wisdom in teaching must be the criteria for choosing the one to be made abbot or prioress even if they are the last in community rank.

May God forbid that a whole community should conspire to elect a prioress or abbot who goes along with its own evil ways. But if it does, and if the bishop of the diocese or any Benedictine leaders or other Christians in the area come to know of these evil ways to any extent, they must block the success of this wicked conspiracy, and set a worthy person in charge of God's house. They may be sure that they will receive a generous reward for this, if they do it with pure motives and zeal for God's honor. Conversely, they may be equally sure that to neglect to do so is sinful.

Merit of life and wisdom of doctrine should determine the choice of the one to be constituted abbot or prioress, even if that monastic be the least senior in the community.

Again, the principles regarding order or rank may seem to be turned upside down. I am part of a monastic community where the last two abbots were under thirty-five when elected. The retired abbot just recently celebrated his fortieth anniversary of benediction as an abbot. His successor was just elected at thirty-four.

What does this tell us about monastic life at the top leadership level? The answer lies in the two emphases spelled out: *merit of life and wisdom of doctrine*, or put another way, *goodness of life and wisdom in teaching*. What constitutes goodness of life? What is wise teaching?

How do these two criteria apply to leadership in recovery? *The good life* is certainly not *la dolce vita* of a filmmaker's fantasy. Nor is it material success or glamorous lifestyle. The *good life* is a sober life, one marked by a constant quest for sobriety and healing from addiction. In my recovery I embrace *the good life* when, as consistently as possible, I try to work the program and practice step four: *examine my life as courageously and as completely as I can.*

And what might *sound teaching* be? Anyone leading a twelve-step group needs to follow the literature closely, without improvising. The closer I stay to the *Big Book* and other approved derivatives, the better. I cannot reinvent the wheel. But I can certainly mess up the steering by imposing my own wisdom, especially if I have a political or religious axe to grind. The scripture "Lean not on thine own understanding" comes to mind here. And as the saying goes, "If it ain't broke, don't fix it." Don't try to fix a program that *works if you work it, and won't if you don't.* The wheel is not crying out to be reinvented.

Lord, if and when I am tapped to lead my recovery community in any capacity, help me model the good life and faithfully teach the tried and true. Amen.

April 21, August 21, December 21

CHAPTER 64: The Election of a Prioress or Abbot
(concluded)

Once in office, the abbot and prioress must keep constantly in mind the nature of the burden they have received, and remember to whom they will have "to give an account of their stewardship" (Luke 16:2). Let them recognize that the goal must be profit for the community members, not preeminence for themselves. They ought, therefore, to be learned in divine law, so that they have a treasury of knowledge from which they can "bring out what is new and what is old" (Matt. 13:52). The abbot and prioress must be chaste, temperate, and merciful, always letting "mercy triumph over judgment" (James 2:13) so that they too may win mercy. They must hate faults but love the members. When they must punish them, they should use prudence and avoid extremes; otherwise, by rubbing too hard to remove the rust, they may break the vessel. They are to distrust their own frailty and remember "not to crush the bruised reed" (Isa. 42:3). By this we do not mean that they should allow faults to flourish, but rather, as we have already said, they should prune them away with prudence and love as they see best for the individual. Let them strive to be loved rather than to be feared.

Excitable, anxious, extreme, obstinate, jealous, or overly suspicious the abbot or prioress must not be. Such a person is never at rest. Instead, they must show forethought and consideration in their orders and whether the task they assign concerns God or the world, they should be discerning and moderate, bearing in mind the discretion of holy Jacob, who said: "If I drive my flocks too hard, they will all die in a single day" (Gen. 33:13). Therefore, drawing on this and other examples of discretion, they must so arrange everything that the strong have something to yearn for and the weak have nothing to run from.

They must, above all, keep this rule in every detail, so that when they have ministered well they will hear from God what that good servant heard who gave the other members of the household grain at the proper time: "I tell you solemnly, God will put this one in charge of greater things" (Matt. 24:47).

Whether one is called to head a religious community, as this *Rule* intends, or whether you and I simply function in the world, interacting with other people, there is plenty of good information here to draw on. Whether I am in charge of other people, as their boss, or whether I am just interacting with peers, I would adapt and personalize three of these pieces of advice Benedict has for his abbots and prioresses.

(1) *Let me exalt mercy above judgment, that I myself may obtain mercy.* There are so many instances in life, especially if I have been mistreated, abused, or neglected, and I remember this, that I can extend a spirit of mercy rather than one of judgment to my offenders. I would hope that when I engage in steps eight and nine, those whom I have offended, or perhaps more than just "offended," might show me more mercy than judgment as well.

(2) *Let me keep my own frailty ever before my eyes and remember that the bruised reed must not be broken.* How often would I have gleefully broken off that "bruised reed" in my face, the person causing me so much discomfort and embarrassment? How quick my temper would flare or my emotions seethe at someone who dared disagree with me or on whom I looked down. When those temptations press, Lord, let me indeed keep my own frailty and my own bruised self before my eyes, and be thankful no one ever snapped me in two or discarded me.

(3) *Let me strive rather to be loved than to be feared.* This one is perhaps the richest, briefest piece of wisdom in this whole section. I am challenged to *study* this, to practice it, to work on it. I am charged with making it my aim to be loved rather than to be feared. In sorrow for sin, there is both imperfect and perfect contrition. I am *imperfectly* sorry if I fear being cast into hell and cut off from God for my sins; I am *perfectly* sorry if I really hate what I did because it hurt and insulted God.

Lord, please teach me to prefer mercy to judgment. Remind me of my own wounded nature, my own frailty, so that others may respond to me in love rather than in fear. And may these signposts be mine. Amen.

April 22, August 22, December 22

CHAPTER 65: The Prior and Subprioress of the Monastery

Too often in the past, the appointment of a subprioress or prior has been the source of serious contention in monasteries. Some, puffed up by the evil spirit of pride and thinking of themselves as a second prioress or abbot, usurp tyrannical power and foster contention and discord in their communities. This occurs especially in monasteries where the same bishop and the same prioress or abbot appoint both the abbot and prioress and the prior or subprioress. It is easy to see what an absurd arrangement this is, because from the very first moment of appointment they are given grounds for pride, as their thoughts suggest to them that they are exempt from the authority of the prioress or abbot. "After all, you were made subprioress or prior by the same members who made the prioress or abbot."

This is an open invitation to envy, quarrels, slander, rivalry, factions, and disorders of every kind, with the result that, while the prioress and subprioress or abbot and prior pursue conflicting policies, their own souls are inevitably endangered by this discord; and at the same time the monastics under them take sides and so go to their ruin. The responsibility for this evil and dangerous situation rests on the heads of those who initiated such a state of confusion.

Power struggles in monasteries? Cloister intrigue and politics? I am afraid so, because for better or for worse, monasteries, like any other institution, are run by human beings, not robots. Competition between abbot and prior or between prioress and subprioress might resemble conflicts between the CEO and the CFO, or the COO in a corporation, each coveting a more powerful upper hand with the board of directors. *Pride goeth before the fall* seems once again to prove itself true.

Holding the office of second-in-command can tempt one to false pride. One begins to engage in deluded thinking and comes to believe that one's power base is not subject to any higher authority. Such a scenario smacks of the scene in the Garden, when Satan is pitching Eve, and ultimately Adam, with the line, *You shall become like gods.* In other words, why respect legitimate authority when you can go grab all the power for yourself?

How do I apply this? Most of us are in one political climate or another where we work. Do I allow myself to get enmeshed in power plays, however petty, or when I get wind of them, do I just choose to back off and pray: *Yours, O Lord, are the power and the victory and the glory and the majesty, for all that is in the heavens and earth are yours. You are the Lord and you are exalted above all.* Amen.

April 23, August 23, December 23

CHAPTER 65: The Prior and Subprioress of the Monastery (concluded)

For the preservation of peace and love we have, therefore, judged it best for the abbot or prioress to make all decisions in the conduct of the monastery. If possible, as we have already established, the whole operation of the monastery should be managed through the deans under the directions of the abbot or prioress. Then, so long as it is entrusted to more than one, no individual will yield to pride. But if local conditions call for it, or the community makes a reasonable and humble request, and the prioress or abbot judges it best, then let them, with the advice of members who reverence God, choose the one they want and themselves make that one the subprioress or prior. The subprioress and prior for their part are to carry out respectfully what the prioress or abbot assigns, and do nothing contrary to their wishes or arrangements, because the more they are set above the rest, the more they should be concerned to keep what the rule commands.

If these subprioresses or priors are found to have serious faults, or are led astray by conceit and grow proud, or show open contempt for the holy rule, they are to be warned verbally as many as four times. If they do not amend, they are to be punished as required by the discipline of the rule. Then, if they still do not reform they are to be deposed from the rank of subprioress or prior and replaced by someone worthy. If after all that, they are not peaceful and obedient members of the community, they should even be expelled from the monastery. Yet the abbot or prioress should reflect that they must give God an account of all their judgments, lest the flames of jealousy or rivalry sear their soul.

The manner of appointing priors or subprioresses has changed since the *Rule* was composed. I know of no recent cases where the local bishop would routinely enter the process. If the bishop does have to get involved in the affairs of a monastery, there must be real trouble brewing. The alternative that Benedict suggests is the one in current usage: *Let the abbot himself or the prioress herself constitute as prior or prioress whomever they shall choose.* Since these persons function essentially as deputies, they must be trustworthy and loyal, especially when the abbot or prioress must be away, which is frequent today.

If the deputy turns out to be given to pride or lusts after power, then the superior holds the ultimate power to depose that deputy and appoint another instead. It has often been said in jest that it's hard to get good help anymore, but sadly enough, that's true.

The discussion about the appointment of worthy priors and subprioresses brings up the whole question of "competent delegation." I can delegate or deputize someone to do something in my behalf, but if I do not make that selection prudently, it will likely backfire on me. The proverbial chickens will come home to roost, probably in a most uncomfortable coop. I need to look at competent delegation under two headings: (1) when I delegate something to be done by another; and (2) when I personally have been delegated to do something for another.

In either scenario, addiction can get in the way if I am not conscientiously working my steps. If I want to make time so I can act out, I might hastily delegate a job to someone else so as to escape my responsibilities and self-medicate through fantasy, alcohol, or some other drug. If, on the other hand, my boss asks me to take on some responsibility in his or her name, then I have a choice: I can rise to that trust and do the job to the best of my ability, or I can do a minimal job, slide by, and steal more time for myself.

Help me, Lord, whether I delegate or am delegated, to be a faithful steward of my time. Help me work my program, so I may be ready when called upon to act responsibly. Amen.

April 24, August 24, December 24

CHAPTER 66: The Porter of the Monastery

At the door of the monastery, place a sensible person who knows how to take a message and deliver a reply, and whose wisdom keeps them from roaming about. This porter will need a room near the entrance so that visitors will always find someone there to answer them. As soon as anyone knocks or a poor person calls out, the porter will reply, "Thanks be to God" or "Your blessing, please," then, with all the gentleness that comes from reverence of God, provide a prompt answer with the warmth of love. Let the porter be given one of the younger members if help is needed.

The monastery should, if possible, be so constructed that within it all necessities, such as water, mill and garden are contained, and the various crafts are practiced. Then there will be no need for the members to roam outside, because this is not at all good for their souls.

We wish this rule to be read often in the community so that none of the members can offer the excuse of ignorance.

At the door of the monastery, place a sensible person who knows how to take a message and deliver a reply. What an insightful opening sentence. Benedict wants to make sure that the first impression someone gets at the monastery door is a good impression. How many receptionists have we encountered who were neither knowledgeable nor reliable? The so-called first line of defense in any enterprise is, for better or for worse, whoever answers the telephone, or whoever answers the door.

Nowadays in larger monasteries, the porter is usually assisted by salaried lay staff. Again, the standard of "competent delegation" comes to mind. It certainly was on Benedict's mind, for he knew an incompetent gatekeeper could wreak havoc on a community. Today, security measures are almost as crucial as they were in the Middle Ages, so this position remains as crucial as ever.

There is a distinctly spiritual character in the role of a porter or a receptionist. The *Rule* directs that *as soon as anyone knocks or a poor person approaches, let the person receiving them respond "Thanks be to God" or "Give me your blessing."* Then, they are to attend to them promptly, with all the meekness inspired by the fear of God and with the warmth of charity.* How beautiful.

In one inner-city abbey in Europe, many poor, homeless, and addicted persons come knocking at the gate. There are so many in need that the abbot raised funds to build a connected facility to distribute food and clothing, to provide medical help and social assistance for this population.

What does this section have to do with you and with me? It sure has to do with how you and I receive people, all kinds of people. Do we give the unattractive, the unwashed, the unlettered the bum's rush? Do we marginalize, ignore, or try to get rid of them? Do we gravitate more toward the beautiful people? That's certainly not Benedict's way. How welcome do I make newcomers feel at twelve-step meetings I attend? Do I offer my phone number? Am I willing to act as a temporary sponsor? I need to examine my conscience. The *Rule* and the Bible suggest I might be encountering Christ or some angel disguised as a beggar.

Lord, help me trace the outline of *your* face in everyone I meet. Let me greet them in my heart, if not with my lips, with the words *"Thanks be to God" or "Give me your blessing, please."* Amen.

CHAPTER 67: Members Sent on a Journey

Members sent on a journey will ask the prioress or abbot and the community to pray for them. All absent members should always be remembered at the closing prayer of the Divine Office. When they come back from a journey, they should, on the very day of their return, lie face down on the floor of the oratory at the conclusion of each of the customary hours of the Divine Office. They ask the prayers of all for their faults, in case they may have been caught off guard on the way by seeing some evil thing or hearing some idle talk.

No monastics should presume to relate to anyone else what they saw or heard outside the monastery, because that causes the greatest harm. If any do so presume, they shall be subjected to the punishment of the rule. So too shall anyone who presumes to leave the enclosure of the monastery, or go anywhere, or do anything at all, however small, without the order of the abbot or the prioress.

Whoever presides at Compline (night prayer) always says a marvelous little prayer *for our sisters or brothers who are absent, that God may protect them.* That custom goes back to this section of the *Rule.* Do we think of praying for family members who are no longer living with us? Sons or daughters who have moved out of the family home? Family or close friends who may be traveling?

This wonderful custom strongly accents family and community, likewise affirming the power of prayer. For those in recovery, prayer is indispensable. Our recovery literature bids us "pray for the man or woman who is still sick." We might well expand that in our meetings, and maybe at our closing prayer, like at Compline, remember *our sisters or brothers who are absent, that God may protect them and keep them sober.*

The other point worth reflecting on in this passage is about gossip. Monastics who return from travels are told not to *presume to tell another whatever they may have seen or heard [of something evil, or through idle talk] outside of the monastery, because this causes very great harm.* Gossip is a dangerous thing. It is an unhealthy thing. It is a toxic thing. I am reminded of something we hear at every meeting: *What you say here, what you hear here, when you leave here, let it stay here.* If we should hear anything unwholesome, bad, sad, or negative—we need not repeat it. Gossip won't help anyone else. It can only scandalize them, which literally means, trip them up.

Lord, help me be a prayerful person who regularly remembers family and friends, sisters and brothers in recovery, especially those absent from meetings. And let me not repeat stories or spread gossip, but let me look for the good, the true, and the beautiful, and share Good News generously. Amen.

April 26, August 26, December 26

CHAPTER 68: Assignment of Impossible Tasks

> Monastics may be assigned a burdensome task or something they cannot do. If so, they should, with complete gentleness and obedience, accept the order given them. Should they see, however, that the weight of the burden is altogether too much for their strength, they should choose the appropriate moment and explain patiently to the prioress or abbot the reasons why they cannot perform the task. This they ought to do without pride, obstinacy or refusal. If after the explanation the abbot or prioress is still determined to hold to their original order, then the junior must recognize that this is best. Trusting in God's help, they must in love obey.

In both the military and religious life, obedience to legitimate authority is a central tenet. Disobeying orders in the military can result in disarray, confusion, and ultimately loss of life. Disobedience in the cloister erodes a core monastic commitment: one's vows, and ultimately one's vocation. But this section talks about when the monastic is ordered to do the impossible. What then? Benedict says to tell the superior gently and charitably that it's beyond the monastic's ability. If the superior persists, then *let the subordinate know that the order is for his or her good, and obey out of love, trusting in the help of God.*

Often, we underrate our own abilities. Most underestimate rather than overestimate their abilities. We more often sell ourselves short. Often our bosses will have more faith in us than we do in ourselves, and thus ask things of us we think are beyond us. An illegal or immoral order, of course, we are never to obey, either in the military or the monastery. There are procedures in both military as well as in canon law to deal with such inappropriate orders. But what about orders that are both legal and moral, yet *we* think lie beyond our capacities?

When I am presented with such an assignment, such a task, I need to reflect: somebody thought I was up to this; were they crazy or what? Or am I just chicken or downright lazy? I may need to stretch, and in stretching may expand my self-imposed horizons.

Lord, please be there when I am asked to perform some task I think is beyond me. I know I can do it, if you will be at my side. At the beginning of every office we say or sing: *O God, come to my help! O Lord, make haste to help me.* May that prayer be on my lips and in my heart when the challenges come. *With my Higher Power, nothing is impossible.* Amen.

April 27, August 27, December 27

CHAPTER 69: The Presumption of Defending Another in the Monastery

> Every precaution must be taken that one member does not presume in any circumstance to defend another in the monastery or to be their champion, even if they are related by the closest ties of blood. In no way whatsoever shall monastics presume to do this, because it can be a most serious source and occasion of contention. Anyone who breaks this rule is to be sharply restrained.

A curious section, this. Normally, we would want to stick up for one another, spring to the defense of a brother or sister under attack or in trouble of some kind, whether a blood relative or just a good friend. But under the vow of obedience in a monastery, things are a lot different than out in the world. Why is there such a section in the *Rule*, and what meaning might it have for us living in the non-cloistered world? The issue is running interference for other people, fighting other people's battles.

The somewhat tired illustration of the overeager Boy Scout comes to mind. Attempting his good deed for the day, he insists on helping a little old lady cross the street. He is all up about doing his duty. But this particular little old lady had absolutely no intention of crossing that particular street. Our scout is out of touch with the larger picture.

When I interfere or impose my agenda on someone else, even with the noblest of intentions, I may just do more damage than good. Like the scout, I may have totally misread the situation. That is why monastics are not to defend other monastics before the superior: they probably don't have all the facts, and bottom line anyway, it's none of their business. It is between the monastic and the superior.

Lord, help me mind my own business. And help me work on surrender. You are always there to help those in distress, and if they want my help, all they have to do is ask. Amen.

April 28, August 28, December 28

CHAPTER 70: The Presumption of Striking Another Monastic at Will

In the monastery every occasion for presumption is to be avoided, and so we decree that no one has the authority to excommunicate or to strike any member of the community unless given this power by the prioress or abbot. "Those who sin should be reprimanded in the presence of all, that the rest may fear" (1 Tim. 5:20). The young up to the age of fifteen should, however, be carefully controlled and supervised by everyone, provided that this too is done with moderation and common sense.

If any member, without the command of the abbot or prioress, assumes any power over those older or, even in the regard to the young, flares up and treats them unreasonably, let that one be subjected to the discipline of the rule. After all, it is written: "Never do to another what you do not want done to yourself" (Tob. 4:16).

Here the *Rule* addresses the issue of meting out discipline in community, how, and by whom. It amplifies somewhat the last section having to do with interfering in community.

This section warns that *every occasion of presumption shall be avoided in the monastery.* I am not to play the overeager scout and proceed to carry out whatever I think needs to be done. Presumption is a form of rash judgment, of drawing hasty conclusions, of shooting from the hip, which generally leads to one catastrophe or another. Minor children are mentioned, since in those days they were living in monasteries alongside adult members of the community, who collectively acted *in loco parentis,* therefore doling out discipline to minors. Hence the injunction that *anyone presuming without the superior's instructions to punish those older than fifteen or who lose their temper with them, shall undergo the discipline of the rule.*

In today's world, I dare not presume or assume anything about anyone, least of all punish them. So-called *humans* can at times be quite *inhumane.* I can also punish someone I have judged by giving them "the silent treatment," freezing them out, ignoring them. Such is one of the cruelest of human behaviors.

Lord, keep my mind and my heart open. Don't let me make rash decisions about what others deserve. Rather, let me surrender to you and commend others to your love and mercy, *for you alone are God, living and true.* Amen.

April 29, August 29, December 29

CHAPTER 71: Mutual Obedience

Obedience is a blessing to be shown by all, not only to the prioress and abbot but also to one another, since we know that it is by this way of obedience that we go to God. Therefore, although order of the prioress and abbot or of the subprioress or prior appointed by them take precedence, and no unofficial order may supersede them, in every other instance younger members should obey their elders with all love and concern. Anyone found objecting to this should be reproved.

If a member is reproved in any way by the abbot or prioress or by one of the elders, even for some very small matter, or gets the impression that one of the elders is angry or disturbed with them, however slightly, that member must, then and there without delay, fall down on the ground at the other's feet to make satisfaction, and lie there until the disturbance is calmed by a blessing. Anyone who refuses to do this should be subjected to corporal punishment or, if stubborn, should be expelled from the monastery.

Monastics are also to obey one another, knowing that by this road of obedience they are going to God. In this instruction, Benedict is expanding on the basic obedience one promises one's religious superior. Though he does not cite it, Ephesians 5:21 supports what he is saying: "Be subject to one another out of reverence for Christ." The notions of gentle mutual correction and of peer accountability are other signs of the equality Benedict is encouraging between fellow monastics. Obedience, literally "deep listening," needs to be lateral as well as vertical in order to foster mutuality within community.

While the "chain of command" is still preserved intact, *giving priority, therefore, to the commands of the superior or deputy superior*, the response to that obedience is expanded. Once again, the respect due senior members of the community surfaces here: *let all juniors obey their seniors with all charity and solicitude*. In this kind of community model, deep, active, and careful listening is encouraged.

Sadly, the art of listening has been lost in our society. Good listening is key to any twelve-step meeting. The protocol demands no cross talk, interrupting, or premature response.

Lord, help me listen more keenly: at meetings, in my family, and at work. Let me be open to consider others' wishes rather than insisting on my own. *Your ways, O Lord, are not my ways.* But if I listen more deeply, I will surely hear your truth on the lips of others. *Speak, Lord, for your servant is listening.* Amen.

April 30, August 30, December 30

CHAPTER 72: The Good Zeal of Monastics

Just as there is a wicked zeal of bitterness which separates from God and leads to hell, so there is a good zeal which separates from evil and leads to God and everlasting life. This, then, is the good zeal which members must foster with fervent love: "They should each try to be the first to show respect to the other" (Rom. 12:10), supporting with the greatest patience one another's weaknesses of body or behavior, and earnestly competing in obedience to one another. No monastics are to pursue what they judge better for themselves, but instead, what they judge better for someone else. Among themselves they show the pure love of sisters and brothers; to God, reverent love; to their prioress or abbot, unfeigned and humble love. Let them prefer nothing whatever to Christ, and may Christ bring us all together to everlasting life.

I love to read texts that have what *Reader's Digest* calls "Quotable Quotes"—succinct sayings pregnant with meaning. They are worthy of embroidery, framing, and display. One line here deserves such honor: *Prefer nothing whatever to Christ.* For the Christian, of course, this line is quotable. But what about those of other persuasions? In recovery, all assent to a Higher Power, however defined.

In the spirit of twelve-step work, let us rephrase Benedict: *Prefer nothing whatever to your Higher Power.* That makes better sense.

Who distinguishes well, teaches well, says an old Latin proverb. Benedict distinguishes between *an evil zeal of bitterness that separates from God and leads to hell, and a good zeal which separates from vices and leads to God and to life everlasting.* "Zeal," kind of an old-fashioned theological word, is still useful, though hard to define in contemporary life. Zeal means that kind of all-out fervor, commitment, energy, and drive that moves to action. Zeal is not zealous unless it has a goal.

Lord, please deliver me from bitter zeal or misdirected energy. Please channel my zeal toward love of you and your values. Let me be consumed with zeal for healing, recovery, and new life, for me as well as my fellow sojourners. Amen.

May 1, August 31, December 31

CHAPTER 73: This Rule Only a Beginning
of Perfection

The reason we have written this rule is that, by observing it in monasteries, we can show that we have some degree of virtue and the beginnings of monastic life. But for anyone hastening on to the perfection of monastic life, there are the teachings of the early church writers, the observance of which will lead them to the very heights of perfection. What page, what passage of the inspired books of the Old and New Testaments is not the truest of guides for human life? What book of the holy writers does not resoundingly summon us along the true way to reach the Creator? Then, beside the *Conferences* of the early church writers, their *Institutes* and their *Lives*, there is also the *Rule of Basil*. For observant and obedient monastics, all these are nothing less than tools for the cultivation of virtues; but as for us, they make us blush for shame at being so slothful, so unobservant, so negligent. Are you hastening toward your heavenly home? Then with Christ's help, keep this little rule that we have written for beginners. After that, you can set out for the loftier summits of the teaching and virtues we mentioned above, and under God's protection you will reach them. Amen.

In completing the last installment of this four-month reading cycle, you now have Benedict's parting words—as we might expect, some important remarks. In crafting his *Rule*, Benedict drew on several previous attempts of others. Benedict wrote for those who would hasten to embrace the kind of life that is meaning*ful*, rather than meaning*less*. Finally, he humbly tacks on a short reading list, should we need more in order to establish a relationship with our Higher Power.

Benedict, editor and compiler *par excellence*, was able to craft both a mighty yet moderate document. In conclusion, he poses the rhetorical question, *What else are all these spiritual sources other than tools of virtue for right-living and obedient people?*

Benedict thought he had written a *minimum rule for beginners*. A minimum *Rule* indeed. What humility and what simplicity. What understatement.

Thank you, Lord, for the gift of Benedict and his gentle beginner's manual for a holy and wholesome life. *Speak, for your servant is listening. Say but the word and my soul shall be healed.* Amen.